MY HEART, HEART, MY LIFE, MY ALL

Some books by William MacDonald

Armageddon Soon?
Believer's Bible Commentary
Christ Loved the Church
Enjoying Ecclesiastes
Ephesians: Mystery of the Church
1 Peter: Faith Tested, Future Triumphant
God's Answers to Man's Questions
Grasping for Shadows
Here's the Difference
Lord, Break Me
Once in Christ, In Christ Forever
True Discipleship
The Wonders of God
Worlds Apart

MY HEART, MY LIFE, MY ALL

Love's Response: A Living Sacrifice

William MacDonald

GOSPEL FOLIO PRESS
304 Killaly St. West Port Colborne, ON L3K 6A6
Available in the UK from
JOHN RITCHIE LTD., Kilmarnock, Scotland

Published by Gospel Folio Press
304 Killaly St. West Port Colborne, ON L3K 6A6

Unless otherwise indicated, Scripture references are from the New King James Version, copyright © 1979, 1980, 1982, 1985 by Thomas Nelson, Inc., Nashville, Tennessee. Used by permission.

Abbreviations

KJV	King James Version
NT	New Translation, J. N. Darby
NASB	New American Standard Bible
NIV	New International Version
NLT	New Living Translation

ISBN 1-882701-44-5

Cover design by J. B. Nicholson, Jr.

Printed in the United States of America

Rick,

He gave the ultimate sacrifice; his heart, his life, his all for us. He asks the same of us, but nothing he hasn't done.

He was and is committed to us. Are we truly committed to him - as he would have us be?

In him,
Corbin

Contents

Part IV: THE HIGH CALLING OF COMMITMENT

Part V: THE EXPERIENCE OF COMMITMENT

Part I
THE LOVE AND LOGIC OF CALVARY

1
The Love and Logic of Calvary

Nothing in the history of the universe can compare with what happened at the place called Calvary. Compressed into a few hours was an event that, as someone said, "towers o'er the wrecks of time."

More books have been published about that event than perhaps any other. More poetry has been written, more sacred music composed. Some of the world's greatest art masterpieces try to picture it. Sermons without number dwell on the subject. It is commemorated worldwide every time a communion service is held. And every time we see a cross, we remember who hung on the best known one. The record of those few hours is told in simple, unemotional language, yet the story never fades or grows old.

It was the day when the Lord Jesus Christ died. His was a death that was unique—unique as to the Person involved, the people for whom it occurred, and the purpose for which it happened. No one, in his wildest imagination, could have ever conceived a story so grand, so awesome, so far-reaching in time and consequences. Brilliant authors have documented unexpected and unlikely stories, but none can ever match the saga of Calvary.

When we try to come to grips with what took place when Christ died, we are faced with tremendous issues. There are conclusions to be drawn, decisions to be made. In the shadow of the cross, we are forced to conclude that it must be everything or nothing. There is no room for neutrality. Those who believe in the Lord Jesus Christ dare not be tepid about His Person and work, lest we insult His majesty and exhibit base ingratitude for what He did. It was with justifiable

11

directness that He said to the church in Laodicea, "So then, because you are lukewarm, and neither cold nor hot, I will vomit you out of My mouth (Rev. 3:16).

People for whom Jesus Christ died cannot deny His just claims on them. Or succumb to a ho-hum Christianity. Or live for selfish pleasure. Our redemption demands our total consecration.

What If...

What would happen if believers could stand before the cross and realize more fully what was really happening there? Overwhelmed by the dimensions of their salvation, they would become compulsive worshipers. They would never stop marvelling at the wonderful grace of Jesus, and would talk about Him to anyone who would listen. Day and night, they would be unashamedly enthusiastic about the One who called them out of darkness into His marvelous light. Worldly ambitions would perish as they gave themselves without reserve to Christ and His service. The world would be evangelized.

Sad to say, this is not the way it is. The church takes it all matter-of-factly. The death of Jesus Christ on the cross of Calvary does not impact us the way it should. Our conceit may even conclude that it was proper that the Son of God should die for us.

Light in Darkness

Every once in a while, a great shaft of light does crash through the darkness. Here and there a believer does stand at Calvary and prays:

> *Oh, make me understand it,*
> *Help me to take it in,*
> *What it meant to Thee, the Holy One,*
> *To bear away my sin.*
>
> —A. M. Kelly

As the deeper significance of what happened there begins to dawn on him or her, that person will never be the same. He says, in effect:

> *I have seen the vision*
> *And for self I cannot live.*
> *Life is worse than worthless*
> *Unless all I give.*
> —Author Unknown

People like that will never again be satisfied with a bland Christian life. They determine that they will never again lower themselves to the chill of their environment. They realize that the Christianity they see every day is not the Christianity of the New Testament. A new drive controls them. They have a passion that absorbs their waking hours. They may become what some call a fanatic, but that does not deter them in the least. If they have lost their mind, they have found the mind of Christ. If they are beside themselves, it is for God. If they seem odd and out-of-step, it is because they march to the beat of a different Drummer. They don't want anything to come between their soul and full commitment to the Saviour.

Four Arresting Facts

What has made these people so different? Four tremendous facts lie behind the change. They have seen who Jesus is, what He has done, who they are by contrast, and the incomparable blessings that flow to them from Calvary.

As we next consider these life-changing truths, let us pray that we, too, will have a deeper appreciation of them and will be committed to Christ more completely than before. It may mean revolutionary changes in our lives. Let us face them bravely and willingly.

2
Who Jesus Is

Now we turn to consider Jesus—who He is. Leave Him out and there can be no straight thinking about the meaning of life. He is the hub of history, the fountain of satisfaction, the embodiment of reality, the central fact of life.

He Is Unique

Jesus is the virgin-born Son of Mary, unique from the outset. Others are born to live; He was born to die. News of a baby's birth usually causes joy; news of His birth troubled the ruler and the local populace. Throughout His life, people were either for Him or against Him. There was no neutrality.

He Is True Man

Jesus was human. He grew hungry, thirsty, and weary. To His contemporaries He seemed normal. In physical appearance, He was one of us. In His twenties, He was a carpenter in Nazareth. At thirty, He began a public ministry of preaching, and teaching. No one had valid reason to doubt His true humanity.

He Is Sinless Man

But there was something that distinguished Jesus' humanity from ours: He was sinless. There was once a Man on this earth who was utterly free from the stain of sin. Never an evil thought, a base motive, a sinful act. He was tempted from without but never from within. He always did those things that pleased His Father—and that precluded the possibility of His ever sinning.

Even people who would not claim to be His friends had to admit that He was innocent. Pilate could find no fault in Him. Pilate's wife spoke of Jesus as a just Man. Herod searched in vain for evidence against Him. The dying thief protested that Jesus had done nothing wrong. The centurion called him a righteous Man. And Judas admitted that he himself had betrayed innocent blood.

Yes, our Lord is unique. He is truly human. And He is sinlessly human, but that is not all. We can never comprehend a fraction of the magnitude of the meaning of Calvary until we realize that the One who died there is more.

He Is God

Yes! The One who died on the middle cross is God Incarnate. Isaiah identified Him as the mighty God (Isa. 9:6). God the Father addressed Him as God: "But to the Son He says: 'Thy throne, O God, is forever and ever....'" (Heb. 1:8). John said "...the Word was God" (John 1:1), then thirteen verses later said, "...and the Word became flesh, and dwelt among us, and we beheld His glory, the glory as of the only begotten of the Father, full of grace and truth"—a description that could apply only to the Lord Jesus. Our Lord insisted that everyone should honor Him just as they honor the Father (John 5:23). Paul spoke of Christ as the One "who is over all, the eternally blessed God" (Rom. 9:5). Over 100 other Scriptures leave no room for argument: Jesus Christ is God. In Him dwells all the fullness of the Godhead bodily (Col. 2:9).

John Wesley caught the wonder of the incarnation when he wrote, "Our God contracted to a span, incomprehensibly made Man." And William Billings, a musical amateur and a tanner by trade, invites us to "Come, see your God extended on the straw."

Another poet, now unknown, wrote: "Lo, within a manger lies He who built the starry skies."

And yet another now anonymous author penned these words:

Cold on the cradle the dewdrops are falling;
Low lies His head with the beasts of the stall.
Angels adore Him, in slumber reclining,
Maker, and Monarch, and Saviour of all.

Booth-Clibborn, a British hymn writer, also realized that it was no less than God who came to Bethlehem:

Down from His glory, ever living story,
*My **God** and Saviour came,*
And Jesus was His name.

The young Jew of Nazareth was the "Ancient of Days." It was God the Son who wore the carpenter's homespun amid the sawdust of that shop. It was the God-man who wore the slave's apron and washed His disciples' feet. It was the Son of God who created optic nerves for a man born blind. No one but God could quell the stormy waters of the Sea of Galilee with a word. Only He could raise a Lazarus after he had been dead four days.

We cannot overemphasize the fact that the Christ of Calvary is the One "who stretches out the heavens, lays the foundation of the earth, and forms the spirit of man within him" (Zech. 12:1). We tend to make Him in our own image and likeness. As He said to His own people in Psalm 50:21, "You thought that I was altogether like you?"

Words are contemptibly inadequate when they try to describe the Person of the Lord Jesus. The mysterious union of God and Man in Him exhausts language. But we mustn't stop there. An added wonder boggles the mind. As we now consider what He did for us, we are overwhelmed by sensory overload.

3
What He Did

If the Person of Christ is a deep that cannot be fathomed, His death on the cross as a Substitute for sinners staggers the imagination. *We have been died for.* And it was not by a man like ourselves. That would be sobering enough, and cause for endless thanksgiving. What we must realize is that the One who gave Himself for us is the Second Person of the Trinity. It's surprising that we aren't more astonished.

But does the Bible really say that God incarnate died for us? Yes, it does. Paul told the Ephesians elders to "shepherd the church of God which He purchased with His own blood" (Acts 20:28).[1] Who purchased the church with His blood? The antecedent of "who" is "God." God was the Buyer, the Church was the purchase, and His blood was the price. The marvel is that the dying Lamb is God in a human body. The One who hung on the cross is the One who inhabits eternity, Immanuel—God with us.

In the first chapter of Colossians, the Spirit dwells at considerable length on the deity of the Lord Jesus Christ; He is the image of the invisible God, the firstborn over all creation (v. 15), the Creator of all things (v. 16), the One who is before all things and in whom all things consist (v.17). Yet in that same context, the Word says, "…in whom we have redemption through His blood, the forgiveness of sins" (v. 14).

Another verse that teaches that it was God in a body of flesh who died on the Cross is Hebrews 1:3: "Who being the brightness of His glory and the express image of His person, and upholding all things by the word of His power, when He had by Himself purged our sins, sat down on the right hand of the Majesty on high." The expression "the brightness of His glory and the express image of His person" means that the Lord Jesus is equal with God the Father in every respect. And it is He who purged our sins when He died at Calvary.

Another strong verse on the deity of Christ is Philippians 2:6. The apostle emphasizes that the Lord Jesus is in the form of God, which means that He is fully God. The Saviour did not think it robbery to be *equal with God.* And yet this same One who is Incarnate God "humbled Himself and became obedient to the point of death, even the death of the cross" (Phil. 2:8).

It is clear, then, that the Person whom men took by lawless hands, and crucified, and put to death is God the Son. In some religions, men, women, and sometimes children die for their god; I never heard of another belief where a divine person dies for his creatures. We never really come to grips with Calvary until we stand before the cross, gaze on the Dearest and Best, and realize that He is God Incarnate, our Creator.

Can God Die?

Such an affirmation raises three questions. First, *God is Spirit* (John 4:24) and a spirit does not have flesh and blood. That is true, but the Son of God clothed Himself in a body of flesh, bones, and blood so that He might purchase the Church.

Second, *God is immortal,* which means that He is not subject to death. How can He die? Again the answer is found in the incarnation. God veiled His deity in a human body so that He might die for humankind. "Jesus…was made a little lower than the angels, for the suffering of death…that He, by the grace of God, might taste death for everyone" (Heb. 2:9).

The Lord Jesus is not God minus something. He is God plus something. That something is humanity. Isaac Watts realized that the One who died for Him was none other than Christ, his God:

> *Forbid it, Lord, that I should boast*
> *Save in the death of Christ, **my God;***
> *All the vain things that charm me most,*
> *I sacrifice them to His blood.*

Charles Wesley faced this fact, then wrote these unforgettable lines:

> *'Tis myst'ry all! **the Immortal dies;***
> *Who can explore His strange design?*
> *In vain the firstborn seraph tries*
> *To sound the depths of love divine.*

The mystery didn't deter Wesley from continuing with the awesome truth:

> *Amazing love! How can it be*
> *That Thou, **my God**, shouldst die for me?*

Who Would Run Things?

A third question arises. If the Upholder of all things died, then who ran the universe during the three days and nights when His body was in the grave? The answer is that when Jesus died, only His body went to the grave. His spirit and soul went to paradise (Luke 23:43), that is, to heaven (2 Cor. 12:2, 4). There was no interval during which He was not in complete control. At one moment, He was on earth, upholding all things by the word of His power. Then immediately He passed to paradise where He continued to control all things without interruption.

The amazing truth that the Supreme Being gave Himself as a sacrifice for us is astounding. The most brilliant efforts to describe it are little more than a stutter. Language hangs its head in shame. It strains the brain to realize that what happened at Calvary was not homicide, the killing of a human by other humans. It was not genocide, the destruction of an ethnic or racial group. It was *deicide,* the murder of deity.

Charles Spurgeon asks: "Who would have thought of *the just Ruler dying for the unjust rebel?* This is no teaching of human mythology, or dream of poetic imagination. This method of explation is known among men only because it is a fact. Fiction could not have devised it. God Himself ordained it. It is not a matter which could have been imagined."

I'm afraid that we develop such deadly familiarity with the words of Scripture that they lose their impact on us. We say, "The Son of God loved me and gave Himself for me," but we neither gasp nor weep. We reel off similar verses with little or no emotion. We preach this truth so blandly and matter-of-factly that it does not bring us or our listeners to their knees. We are guilty of what someone called the curse of a dry-eyed Christianity. Constantly we need to come back to the awesome reality that it was our Saviour-God who died for us.

F. W. Pitt captures something of the wonder of it all in these memorable lines:

> *The Maker of the universe*
> *As man for man was made a curse;*
> *The claims of law which He had made,*
> *Unto the uttermost He paid.*
> *His holy fingers made the bough*
> *Which grew the thorns that crowned His brow.*
> *The nails that pierced His hands were mined*
> *In secret places He designed;*
> *He made the forest whence there sprung*
> *The tree on which His body hung.*
> *He died upon a cross of wood,*
> *Yet made the hill on which it stood.*
> *The sky that darkened o'er His head*
> *By Him above the earth was spread;*
> *The sun that hid from Him its face*
> *By His decree was poised in space;*
> *The spear that spilled His precious blood*
> *Was tempered in the fires of God.*

The grave in which His form was laid
Was hewn in rock His hands had made;
The throne on which He now appears
Was His from everlasting years;
But a new glory crowns His brow,
And every knee to Him shall bow.

The marvel of the death of the One who hurled the farthest galaxies into space increases still more when we now consider the kind of people for whom He died. It is not a pretty picture.

ENDNOTE

1 This could also be translated "with the blood of His own," meaning God's own Son. J. N. Darby gives it this meaning in his New Translation.

4
Who We Are

The whole divine program of redemption becomes even more astounding when we think of the people for whom the Lord died, the ones He purchased with His own blood (Acts 20:28). I am speaking, of course, of ourselves and the whole human race.

Insignificant

In the universe scanned by the Hubble telescope, we are microscopically tiny. We live on a planet that is not exactly the biggest thing that God has made. In fact, our earth is not more than a speck of cosmic dust, which means that we are microscopic midgets on a speck of cosmic dust. A physicist said that humans are "mere self-replicating specks of matter trapped on a tiny planet for a few dozen orbits about an undistinguished star in one of billions of galaxies."[1] The realization of our insignificance brought forth from the psalmist the breathless question, "What is man that Thou art mindful of him, and the son of man that Thou visitest him?" (Ps. 8:4, KJV).

Frail

Not only are we minuscule, we are frail mortals, made of nothing more substantial than dust and water. One day we are in full athletic strength, but in a few hours we are laid low by some non-filterable virus. One moment we are able to cope with problems as they arise. Then in the face of some accident or sickness, we become emotional basket cases.

Perishable

We are transient. In the light of eternity, our life on earth hardly registers on the time scale. Our poets have likened human life to a breath, a swift ship, an eagle's dive, a shadow, a handbreadth, a sleep. Life is like smoke, vapor, grass, flowers, a weaver's shuttle. Spurgeon reduced our biography to four one-syllable words: Sown. Grown. Blown. Gone.

Evil

Still worse is the fact that we are really not nice people. That is probably the understatement of the century. We are all sinners, and sin has affected every part of our being. Although we may not have committed every sin in the book, we are capable of it. We are shocked by the behavior of others, yet we forget that we are capable of worse. What we are is worse than anything we have done. Our potential for evil is monstrous. The prophet Jeremiah reminded us that the heart of man is "deceitful above all things, and desperately wicked" (Jer. 17:9). Not one of us fully realizes the depth of our personal depravity.

Unclean

Bildad, one of Job's so-called comforters, gave us the ultimate put-down when he argued that if, as far as God is concerned, "the moon does not shine, and the stars are not pure in His sight, how much less man, who is a maggot, and the son of man, who is a worm" (Job. 25:5-6). Isaiah was somewhat more delicate when he said that the inhabitants of the earth are like grasshoppers to Him who sits above the circle of the earth (Isa. 40:22).

God-haters

In our unconverted days, we did not love God with all our soul, mind, heart, and strength. Rather, we said, "Depart from us, for we do not desire the knowledge of Thy ways" (Job 21:14, KJV). It often made us uncomfortable to think about God. With others, we were ashamed to talk about Him. We can remember times when we were happy only when we could forget Him, and sad only when we remembered Him. No cosmic deity was going to run our lives! To be blunt about it, we were at war with Him. In the words of Major André.[2]

> *Against the God who built the sky,*
> *We fought with hands uplifted high;*
> *Despised the mention of His grace,*
> *Too proud to seek a hiding place.*

Murderers

We never know the wickedness of the human heart, however, until we stand before the cross of Calvary and watch man killing the Lord of Glory. The thought is overwhelming, breathtaking, unimaginable. God the Son comes to earth to rescue His creatures, and they turn on Him and kill the One on whom their very existence depends.

Of course, that was not the end. He rose from the dead and later ascended to heaven. Ever since then, He has been offering eternal life as a free gift to all who will repent of their sins and receive Him as Lord and Saviour, believing that, as their Substitute, He died to pay the penalty of their sins.

That is what grace means. God could have turned His back on the human race. He could have vaporized them in a nuclear holocaust. No one would have been left to accuse Him of injustice. Instead, He chose to populate heaven with those who spat in His face and nailed Him to a cross.

Forgetful and Unmoved

If we constantly remembered that the Christ of Calvary is the God of eternity, we would be "lost in wonder, love, and praise." "Here full hearts could only weep, drowned in mercy's glorious deep" (Anon). It would be such an astonishment to us that we would want to share it with everyone we met in endless wonderment. We would not want to talk about anything else. It would bow

27

us in worship, compel us in service, and motivate us in witness. But we don't remember. We commit the awful sin of taking it all for granted.

Have we not lost the titanic wonder of it all? We have recited the scriptures so often and so mechanically that they have become dull for us. The older we get, the harder it is to maintain our earlier amazement. Too often we have to ask:

> *Am I a stone, and not a sheep,*
> *That I can stand, O Christ, beneath Thy cross,*
> *And number, drop by drop,*
> *Thy blood's slow loss,*
> *And yet not weep?*
>
> —Christina Rossetti

Too often we have to admit:

> *Oh, wonder to myself I am,*
> *Thou loving, bleeding, dying Lamb,*
> *That I can scan the myst'ry o'er*
> *And not be moved to love Thee more.*
>
> —Anonymous

J. H. Jowett marveled at our insensibility. He wrote:

We leave our places of worship, and no deep and inexpressible wonder sits upon our faces. We can sing those lilting melodies, and when we go out into the streets, our faces are one with the faces of those who have left the theaters and the music halls. There is nothing about us to suggest that we have been looking at anything stupendous and overwhelming…And what is the explanation of the loss? Preeminently our impoverished conception of God.[3]

We must recapture the immensity of Calvary: the Suffering Saviour is the omnipotent, omniscient, omnipresent Lord of Glory, God manifest in the flesh.

ENDNOTE

1   Quoted in *U. S. News and World Report,* August 18, 1997, p. 85.

2   This is a verse of a poem *My Hiding Place* generally attributed to John André, a British major in the American Revolution. Because he met with Benedict Arnold, he was executed as a spy. There is a monument on the spot where he was executed at Tappan, New York, that bears this tribute by General George Washington: "He was more unfortunate than criminal. An accomplished man and gallant officer."

3   Quoted from *The Ministry of a Transfigured Life* in *Christianity Today,* July 14, 1997, p. 56.

5
His Pain, Our Gain

Now consider the incomparable benefits that have come to us through Christ.

We Are Saved

First of all, the Lord Jesus has saved us from hell, from the lake of fire. It is fire that is unquenchable and everlasting. Concerning the inhabitants of hell, Jesus said, "Their worm does not die and the fire is not quenched" (Mark 9:44). In other words, their mental anguish and physical suffering are unending. Hell means separation from God. It is existence in the blackness of darkness forever. It means to be in a place where there is no love. If the Lord Jesus had done no more than save believers from that fate, that in itself would have been cause for endless gratitude and worship. But He did more.

We Are Forgiven

Our sins are forgiven. All of them. Since Christ paid the penalty, God can righteously pronounce us forgiven when we repent and receive His Son as our Lord and Saviour. Our sins are gone as far as the east is from the west, buried in the sea of eternal forgetfulness, blotted out as a thick cloud, cast behind God's back, cast into the depths of the sea, and made white as snow. His forgiveness is so effective that He cannot find a single sin on us for which to punish us with eternal death. As sinners, we receive judicial forgiveness of sins when we believe on Christ. As believers, we receive parental forgiveness when we confess our sins.

We Receive Eternal Life

God gives us eternal life. This is more than endless existence. It means that we receive the life of Christ, a new quality of life. We become "partakers of His divine nature" (2 Pet. 1:4). All things become new—a new hatred of sin; a new love of holiness; a new love of one's fellow believers; a new love for the world of lost people; a new freedom from the dominion of sin; a new life of righteousness; and a new desire to confess Christ.

We Are Accepted

As long as we were in our sins, we had no right to enter God's presence. We were unclean, unholy, and unworthy. But the moment we are born again, God sees us in Christ and accepts us on that basis. As C. D. Martin said in his hymn, *Accepted in the Beloved:*

> *God sees my Saviour and then He sees me*
> *"In the Beloved," accepted and free.*

As to our standing before God, we are clothed in Christ, enveloped in the Son of God's love. A beggar can't enter a ruler's presence in his own worthiness (he probably has none). But the royal prince could take him into the court and introduce him to the monarch. In that case, he is accepted by virtue of the one in whose name he comes. The Lord Jesus is our Royal Prince who has opened the way to the Father for us.

We Are Complete

In ourselves we are not fit for heaven, either before or after conversion. God's standard is perfection and we cannot reach it. Neither by good works nor by a virtuous life can we qualify to be citizens of heaven. But one of the wonderful things that happens when we accept Christ is that God hereafter links us with His Son. He places us in Christ. The Lord Jesus then becomes our fitness for God's presence. We are "complete in Him" (Col. 2:10). If we have Him, we don't need anything else to make us eligible. It is what He has done, not what we must do that counts. It is His merit, not ours. It is because the Father sees us in Him that we are qualified to be "partakers of the inheritance of the saints in the light" (Col. 1:12). We are as fit for heaven as God Himself can make us because Christ is our fitness and He cannot be improved on.

We Are Children of God

At the moment of conversion, we are born into the family of God. From then on He is our Father and we are His children in a relationship that cannot be broken. No angel is so privileged. It is reserved for sinners saved by grace. Whether we study the starry universe through a telescope or a living cell through a microscope, we can say, "My Father made it all." Worldlings may boast of their ancestry, their links to the famous, or their ties to the wealthy. But all these honors are tawdry compared to knowing God personally as Father.

We Are Heirs and Joint Heirs

Because we are His children, we are heirs of God and joint heirs with Jesus Christ. This means—hold your hat—that all God has is ours. The apostle Paul said, "All things are yours...and you are Christ's and Christ is God's" (1 Cor. 3:21-22). Right away we are tempted to think in terms of material wealth, but that is probably the least of it. Paul explains the "all things" as including God's servants (you don't have to choose one above the other), the world, life, death, things present, or things to come. It is safe to say that our minds are incapable of fathoming all that is involved in being heirs of God, but one day we will come into the full enjoyment of it all.

In the meantime, we can revel in the fact that we sinners, saved by grace, are now inheritors of all the divine treasury. There is no Cinderella story like this, no rise from such rags to such riches. It is enough to blow fuses in our brains.

33

We Are Indwelt

The Holy Spirit indwells every believer. Just think of it: The Third Person of the Trinity actually inhabits our lowly bodies. He is there as a seal, marking us out as eternally belonging to God. He is a down payment, guaranteeing that we will receive all that the Saviour purchased for us at Calvary, including the glorified body.

As the anointing, He enables us to discern truth and error. He is a helper, drawing near to assist in times of need. He guides us, prays for us, and produces the fruit of holiness in our lives. We may well ask, "What good and needed ministry does He not perform for us?"

We Are His Bride

The Church, made up of all believers, is the bride of Christ. This speaks of the special love He has for us. "Christ loved the Church and gave Himself for it, that He might sanctify and cleanse it with the washing of water by the word, that He might present it to Himself a glorious Church, not having spot or wrinkle or any such thing, but that it should be holy and without blemish" (Eph. 5:25-27).

To be a part of His bride is a greater honor than membership in all the prestigious organizations, fraternities, and societies of earth. The Church means more to God than all the nations of the world. They are only a drop in the bucket or dust on the scale (see Isa. 40:15). The Church is the bride of Christ. It is the fellowship of the excellent of the earth.

We Are Able to Pray

We have constant access to the Sovereign of the universe in prayer. No appointment is necessary. By faith, we enter the most holy place with our worship, praise, and thanksgiving, then with our supplications and intercessions. We know that He answers every prayer in exactly the same way we would if we had His wisdom, love, and power. This privilege of prayer was bought for us by the blood of Jesus (Heb. 10:19), and is of priceless value.

34

We Will Have Eternal Glory

We are destined to eternal glory with the Lord in heaven. The Saviour was not satisfied to save us from hell, or to give us prolonged existence on Planet Earth. No, He will not be fully satisfied until we receive glorified bodies like His own resurrection body, and are with Him in heaven.

> *And is it so—I shall be like Thy Son?*
> *Is this the grace which He for me has won?*
> *Father of glory, thought beyond all thought!*
> *In glory, to His own blest likeness brought!*
> —J. N. Darby

After we have said all this, we have not scratched the surface of the blessings that flow to us from the cross. Paul sums it up by saying that we have been blessed "with every spiritual blessing in the heavenly places in Christ" (Eph. 1:3). We are the most favored people on earth, and it is all because of Calvary. His pain is truly our gain.

We Need to Respond

There is only one conclusion. As we have said, it must be everything for Christ or nothing. No longer can we fritter our lives away in trivial pursuits. No longer can we be content to be what J. H. Jowett called "minor officials in transient enterprises." Henceforth we must determine that love so amazing, so divine *will have* "our hearts, our lives, our all." We must make a total commitment of ourselves to Him.

Part II
COMMITMENT
AS SEEN IN SCRIPTURE

6
What is Commitment?

The logic of our redemption has led us down a one-way street that should end in total commitment.[1] Okay. Does that mean that my obligation is to attend church regularly, put money in the collection, read the Bible from time to time, and pray? Is that all it means? Hardly.

Commitment is a definite, well-considered act in which a person turns his or her life over to the Lord so that He can do whatever He wants with it. It is exchanging our will for His. It is giving up our rag-rights and acknowledging His throne-rights. It is abandoning all for the One who abandoned all for us.

In every life there is a throne. The natural occupant of that throne is self. Commitment is when that self is dethroned and the Lord Jesus is crowned King. It is when we say from our hearts:

> *Take me as I am, Lord,*
> *And make me all Thine own;*
> *Make my heart Thy palace*
> *And Thy royal throne.*
>
> —Anonymous

It is possible to commit my life to Jesus for salvation, yet fall short of committing it to Him for service. Both commitments should happen at conversion, as they did with Saul of Tarsus, but regrettably things are not always what they should be in this life.

Commitment is denying self, taking up the cross, and following

Him. It is losing one's life for His sake and the gospel's. It is flinging one's soul and body down for God to plow them under. When you desire His will supremely and are giving Him the devotion of your heart and the love of your soul, you are a committed Christian.

Unconditional Surrender

All-out dedication to Jesus is unconditional. Certain words or phrases are not in its vocabulary, like "Not so, Lord," "I will follow You, but let me first...," "Not now, but later." Commitment means submission to Him in sickness or health, in poverty or plenty, at home or overseas, single or married, unknown or well-known, a short life or a long one.

Does this seem like a heavy load to lay on a person? On the contrary, Christ said that His yoke is easy and His burden is light. What is really hard is trying to chart one's own course and do one's own thing.

ENDNOTE

1   There may be a valid question whether any believer is *totally* committed to the Saviour. Even the apostle Paul had to admit that he had not already attained, or was already perfected (Phil. 3:12). When we think of our sins, failures, self-centeredness, and mixed motives, we hesitate to claim that our dedication to the Lord is what it should be. And yet that should not stop us from striving toward the ideal. Even if we have not arrived, we can still press toward the goal. Even if we can't sing, "All to Jesus I surrender" as our present experience, we can sing it as the aspiration of our heart. And although we may never realize total commitment, we can seek to maximize the extent to which our lives are turned over to the Lord.

7

The Commitment of Christ

Just as our Lord is the author and finisher of faith, so He is the inventor and chief example of commitment. To know what is meant by that word, we study the life of the Son of God.

When the Father looked down on our lostness and desperate need, He called for a volunteer: "Whom shall I send, and who will go for Us?" The only One who was qualified was also willing. "Here I am. Send Me," the Son said, in essence. He wanted to do the will of God, and He knew exactly what that meant.

It meant for the Creator to be born in a stable. Not for Him an antiseptic maternity ward or a clean bassinet. No. A smelly cattle shed and the straw of a feed box for a mattress would have to do.

Even in later years, our Lord knew nothing of the comforts that we consider inalienable rights. He never had hot and cold running water, bathroom facilities, or an inner-spring mattress. He did not have what even foxes and birds have, a resting place of His own. While His disciples dispersed to their homes, Jesus slept out on the Mount of Olives. As E. S. Elliott wrote, "Thy bed was the sod, O Thou Son of God."

The Saviour knew that the will of God meant coming into a world of sin. We cannot know the suffering that this advent caused His sinless soul. He was repulsed and revolted by sin. It causes us pain to resist temptation; it caused the Sinless One profound suffering even to come into contact with it.

41

Sweet Injuries?

In accepting the will of God, our Saviour knew that He would be despised and rejected. He would pour out His life, showering blessing on people. He would give sight to the blind, hearing to the deaf, and deliverance to the demon-possessed. The mute would speak, the lame would walk, and dead people would live again. Yet He would receive ingratitude and abuse.

> *Why, what hath my Lord done?*
> *What makes this rage and spite?*
> *He made the lame to run,*
> *He gave the blind their sight.*
> *Sweet injuries!*
> *Yet they at these*
> *Themselves displease,*
> *And 'gainst Him rise.*
>
> —Samuel Crossman

Jesus knew what loneliness was, and was well acquainted with grief. He earned the name *Man of Sorrows*. He would be insulted, accused of being born of fornication, of being demon possessed, of performing miracles in the power of the Devil—all by His own creatures. But did He think of turning back? Never.

> *It was a lonely path He trod,*
> *From every human soul apart.*
> *Known only to Himself and God*
> *Was all the grief that filled His heart;*
> *Yet from the track He turned not back*
> *Till, where I lay in sin and shame,*
> *He FOUND ME! Blessed be His Name!*
>
> —Author Unknown

When the Son said, "Here I am. Send Me," the future was an open book to Him. But He was so committed to the Father's will that He faced it with determination.

42

Time after time, in His earthly ministry, He spoke of His desire to be totally committed to His God and Father. He appealed to the consistent testimony of the Word that His purpose in coming into the world was to do His Father's will (Heb. 10:7). When He cleansed the temple, His disciples remembered Psalm 69:9: "...zeal for Thy house has eaten me up." Commitment to His Father's interests consumed the Saviour.

When, as a boy, His parents rebuked Him for absenting Himself from the caravan returning to Nazareth, He reminded them that He had to be about His Father's business (Luke 2:49). When the disciples expressed concern that He hadn't eaten recently, He said, "My food is to do the will of Him who sent Me and to finish His work" (John 4:34).

In saying, "The Son can do nothing of Himself (John 5:19), the Lord disclaimed any initiative or originality in His actions. Everything He did was in obedience to the Father (John 7:16; 12:50; 14:10, 31). To those who sought to kill Him because He healed on the Sabbath, He said, "I do not seek My own will, but the will of the Father who sent Me" (John 5:30b). No one had ever been so focused. One day He said to the multitude, "For I have come down from heaven, not to do My own will, but the will of Him who sent Me" (John 6:38). Under similar circumstances, He said to His would-be assassins, "I always do those things that please Him" (John 8:29b). Obedience was not an occasional act; it was the story of His life.

The shadow of the cross was always before Him, but He faced it calmly—and even with eagerness. "I have a baptism to be baptized with," He said, "and how distressed I am till it is accomplished" (Luke 12:50). There was no shrinking back. On the final, fateful trip to Jerusalem, He "went on ahead" (Luke 19:28). It seems that the disciples lagged behind, dragging reluctant feet.

The will of God would include Gethsemane where He prayed, "O My Father, if it is possible, let this cup pass from Me; nevertheless, not as I will, but as Thou wilt" (Mt. 26:39, KJV). His anguished cry was not for escape from death. Rather it was for a divine indication that we could be saved in no other way. His rhetorical question whether there was another way was answered by the silence of heaven. There was no other way.

Denied, Betrayed, Forsaken

Jesus would be betrayed by a friend, denied by a weak disciple, kissed by a Satan-possessed man, and forsaken by those closest to Him. He would be arrested on trumped-up charges and judged in a trial that was the ultimate farce. The verdict would be "Not guilty," yet He would be sentenced to die. He could have called down more than twelve legions of angels, but He chose to die—for you and for me. He preferred the will of God to His own safety.

He had power to come down from the cross, but He had power not to come down. He did not want to be saved from it. It was for this hour that He had come into the world (John 12:27). It was not the nails that held Him there, but His commitment to the will of God.

Sin-bearing Substitute

The greatest horror would be in those three hours of darkness when God would forsake His Son, when the Lord Jesus would bear the undiluted wrath of God to pay the penalty of our sins. No finite mind will ever be able to comprehend what this meant to the Holy One. But He was willing to endure it in obedience to the will of God and out of love for our souls.

Yes, He knew that He would rise from the dead, ascend back to heaven, and be honored with the Name that is above every name. He knew that eventually every knee would bow to Him and every tongue confess Him as Lord. But before the crown was the cross; before the glory the sufferings. The Lord Jesus was totally committed to the will of God whatever the cost might be.

Our Saviour was committed to God, and He has left us an example that we should follow His steps. Whenever we are tempted to complain or retreat, we should call on Him to "nerve our faint endeavor."

44

Lord, when I am weary with toiling,
And burdensome seem Thy commands,
If my load should lead to complaining,
Lord, show me Thy hands,
Thy nail-pierced hands, Thy cross-torn hands,
My Saviour, show me Thy hands.

Christ, if ever my footsteps should falter,
And I be prepared for retreat,
If desert or thorn cause lamenting,
Lord, show me Thy feet,
Thy bleeding feet, Thy nail-scarred feet,
My Jesus, show me Thy feet.

—Anonymous

8
An Early Call

Nowhere in the Bible is the call to total commitment more explicit and inescapable than in Deuteronomy 6:5—

You shall love the Lord your God with all your heart, with all your soul, and with all your strength.

Lest anyone object that this belongs to the legal dispensation and thus doesn't apply to us today, the Holy Spirit repeats it three times in the New Testament, adding "with all your mind" (Mt. 22:37; Mark 12:30; Luke 10:27). In the Gospels, however, this call is not given as law with a penalty attached, but as instruction in righteousness for those who are saved by grace.

Jesus said that loving God is the first and great commandment. Then He added that on two commandments (love God and love your neighbor) hang all the Law and the Prophets, that is, they summarize the entire Old Testament. Because these two laws are more than all the Hebraic system of sacrifices, they must be of more than passing importance for us. The commandment sets the standard for us and shows us how far we fall short.

It is also a call to commitment. Even though we cannot obey it perfectly, we should be moving in that direction. For us on earth, it will never be an achievement, but it should always be an on-going process.

"You shall love the Lord your God..." He is our Lord, our Master. He is our God, our Creator, Sustainer, Saviour, and Preserver. He deserves our love, and when He has it, He will also have our obedience.

Our Affectionate Powers

"With all your heart..." Our God must have first place in our heart. Any other love must be secondary. Don't pass over the word *all* here and in the following expressions. Here it means to love the Lord supremely.

What will it be like when we love Him? We get a clue when we study the affectionate relationship between the Shulamite maiden and her lover in the Song of Solomon.

- She was never more happy than when she was in his presence.
- His absence pained her. She longed for him to come.
- She talked about him with great delight. Her tongue was "the pen of a ready writer."
- She loved to talk to him. Sometimes even when he was not present, she spoke to him out loud.
- She was always pleased to hear his voice.
- She dreamed about him, and relished every memory of him.
- There were no competitors for her love.
- He was the object of her affections.

That's the way it should be between us and the Lord.

Our Emotional Powers

"With all your soul..." Since the soul is the seat of the emotions, we are justified in understanding this to mean that we should love God with all our emotional powers. We should be enthusiastic about Him, joyful when we hear Him exalted, and angry at anything that dishonors Him. When we remember Him, joy and sorrow are mingled—joy to know that His sufferings are over, and sorrow that it was our sins that caused them.

Our Intellectual Powers

"With all your mind..." This phrase calls us to give the best of our intellectual powers to the Lord. We should take our mind, and, as it were, lay it adoringly at His feet, asking Him to use it for His glory. One way we can do that is by saturating our mind with the Scriptures so that we can first of all obey it ourselves, and then minister it to others. We all face the choice of giving our best to the world or to the Lord. Better to be known as a person of the Word than a person of the world.

Our Physical Powers

"With all your strength..." We should love the Lord with all our physical powers. It is good for us to remember that He "does not delight in the strength of the horse; He takes no pleasure in the legs of a man. The Lord takes pleasure in those who fear Him, in those who hope in His mercy" (Ps. 147:10-11).

Prowess in spiritual things counts for more than popularity on the athletic field. A former athlete said, "The biggest thrill of my life was when I first scored the decisive goal in a big match and heard the roar of the cheering crowds. But in the quiet of my room that night, a sense of the futility of it all swept over me. After all, what was it worth? Was there nothing better to live for than to score goals?"

Those who live for this world's honors are selling their birthright for a bowl of chili. Imagine giving one's best for a ribbon, a plaque, a gold cup. One man who lived for these things said, "The dream of the reality was better than the reality of the dream."

Young people who want to obey the first and great commandment cannot express their resolve better than in the words of Thomas H. Gill:

> *Lord, in the fullness of my might,*
> *I would for Thee be strong;*
> *While runneth o'er each dear delight,*
> *To Thee should soar my song.*

49

I would not give the world my heart,
And then profess Thy love;
I would not feel my strength depart,
And then Thy service prove.

I would not with swift wingéd zeal,
On the world's errands go;
And labor up the heavenly hill,
With weary feet and slow.

O not for Thee my weak desires,
My poorer, baser part;
O not for Thee my fading fires,
The ashes of my heart.

O choose me in my golden time,
In my dear joys have part;
For Thee, the glory of my prime,
The fullness of my heart.

The commandment to love God with all the heart, soul, and strength is partially echoed in the last book of the Bible where the hosts of heaven say with a loud voice, "Worthy is the Lamb who was slain to receive power and riches and wisdom and strength and honor and glory and blessing!" (Rev. 5:12). Yes, the Saviour already has all power and riches and wisdom and strength and honor and glory and blessing. But the thought here is that He is worthy to receive all these things from you and from me. Certainly that includes our intellectual powers (wisdom), our physical powers (strength), and our emotional powers (honor and glory and blessing).

There is no question that He is worthy of our finest powers. The only question is, "Will He have them?"

9
Abraham

The Old Testament abounds in examples of commitment. Dedicated men and women cross the stage of history, drawing us to admire their staunch devotion. One person in whom we see outstanding dedication is Abraham. His obedience to the will of God shines out in His willingness to offer Isaac.

It started at Beersheba, about fifty miles southwest of Jerusalem. Abraham was living there with his family. The city was on a trade route linking Egypt with Hebron, Bethlehem, and points north.

The day had begun like most other days. There was no indication that anything momentous would happen, that history would be made, that the ordinary routine of life would be broken. Then Abraham heard Someone call his name.

"Abraham."

"I'm here," he replied.

A Heart-rending Order

Then came an extraordinary command. "Take your son, your only son Isaac, whom you love, and go to the land of Moriah, and offer him as a burnt offering on one of the mountains there. I'll tell you which one" (see Gen. 22:2).

There was no question who was speaking. It was the Lord. And there was no misunderstanding what He said. It was about the patriarch's only son, his unique son, his son of special birth. Abraham was one hundred years old when Isaac was born and Sarah was ninety-one. This was the son through whom God had promised to raise up a numberless posterity and to bless all nations.

Isaac was perhaps twenty-five, and still unmarried. Yet God was commanding Father Abraham to offer him as a burnt offering. Jehovah even specified the place, one of the mounts of the Moriah ridge.

The message was shocking. Never before had the Lord sanctioned human sacrifice, yet now He was commanding it. It seemed that Jehovah was plunging a knife into four successive layers of Abraham's heart. He didn't just say, "Your son," but then "Your only son." Not content with that, God named the son, "Isaac," and then the final agony, "whom you love." "Your son, your only son, Isaac, whom you love."

Unquestioning Obedience

But this was no time for questions. No time for arguing with God. No time to ask for a delay. Abraham had received his order, and he was ready to obey. In preparation, he doubtless turned in early for a good night's rest. (How could any father rest under those circumstances?)

By dawn's light, he was awake. There was the donkey to be saddled, the knife to be honed, the axe to be sharpened, and wood to be split for a burnt offering. Everything but an animal for the sacrifice. The two young servants had to be readied. And, oh yes, Isaac. There could be no journey without him.

Perhaps it was good that Abraham was kept busy. There was no time to think of what lay ahead. Plenty of time for that in the hours that would follow. Humanly speaking, that father's feet should have been as heavy as lead. But for some reason they weren't. He seemed to be propelled by a special inflow of strength and grace.

So they set out on a trip that would take three or more days. It was then that Abraham's mind started racing. Surely he felt a tangled mass of conflicting emotions. How long he had waited for God's promise of a son to be fulfilled! How he had almost burst with pride and satisfaction when the baby was born. How he had

52

watched the child grow, doting on him with affection too great for words.

And he thought of God's promise. Descendants as numerous as the stars of heaven and the sands of the seaside. They would become a great and mighty nation, and all the nations of the earth would be blessed in his seed. Isaac was the one through whom the line would pass.

Now, God had told Abraham to kill Isaac. That would nullify the promises. How could they be fulfilled if Isaac were to die unmarried? Even if the patriarch could have another son, it wouldn't work because God had said, "In Isaac shall your seed be called."

Oceans of Emotion

It is understandable if the old man was quiet for most of the trip, if for three days he hardly spoke a word. The donkey plodded on, carrying the loving father toward the place of destiny. Surely he anguished over the impending death of Isaac. Every time he sneaked a look at his fine son, his eyes doubtlessly misted. He dared not look too long.

But then he would think about the Lord. After all, God had made these promises, and nothing is more sure than the word of God. If He says it, it will come to pass. He cannot lie. He cannot deceive; He cannot be deceived. So what seems impossible to man is possible with God. If God has promised a numerous posterity through Isaac, and if He commands that Isaac be slain, then there is only one solution; He will raise him from the dead.

Perhaps Abraham was startled by the audacity of his own faith. He had never heard of resurrection before. But knowing God as he did, Abraham realized that it was a moral necessity.

Are we justified in thinking that at night he slept close to Isaac, reaching over to touch his shoulders, making sure that he was there, cherishing these last hours together?

Now they have passed Hebron, and now they have left Bethlehem behind. Over rolling landscape, with rock-strewn fields on either side, Abraham set his face with grim determination.

On to Moriah

On the third day, they came to the brow of a hill, one that could appropriately be called "Heartbreak Hill." There, for the first time, they could look to the north and see ocher-tinted buildings just beneath the southern flank of Mount Moriah. That is where Abraham would face the greatest test of his life. There Isaac would be slain and totally consumed by fire in an act of worship to God. Surely Abraham's chest heaved. Surely Isaac noticed it, but said nothing.

Finally, the father broke the silence. Turning to the two young men, he said, "You stay here with the donkey. I and my son will go to Mount Moriah to worship—but we will come back to you."

What is this? *"We* will come back to you?" Didn't he mean, *"I* will come back to you?" No, he knew what he was saying. *"We* will come back to you."

For some reason, that father and son had to walk the remaining miles alone. No one else can share in the poignancy of the last segment of the trip. Abraham picked up the pile of wood and tied it to Isaac's back. That left the torch of fire and the knife for him to carry. All the components of a living sacrifice.

Was there animated conversation between the old man and his lithe, athletic son? We do not know. But there is no suggestion of complaint, of reluctance, of foot-dragging. There seems to be no thought of turning back. Both press on. It is all so incredible, so unreal.

The Supreme Test of Faith

Finally, Isaac asked the unsettling question. "Father, the wood and the fire are here, but where is the lamb for a burnt offering?" Apparently Isaac didn't understand the real purpose of the trip until then. But Abraham knew, and the question cut down into the deepest parts of his being. But once again faith triumphed over human emotions. Abraham deflected the sharpness of the question by assuring his son that God would provide for Himself a lamb for a burnt offering.

At last they came to the designated place. Abraham gathered a pile of rocks, forming them into the shape of an altar. Then he placed the wood on top. Then that father, who loved God supremely, actually tied up his son and laid him on top of the wood. That old man, his hands probably shaking, was given strength to pick up his adult son and place him on the altar. Equally astonishing is that the son, who could have easily overpowered his aged father, submitted without protest.

No artist could do justice to this scene. Here is a father ready to offer his son to God. Here is an innocent son about to die in obedience to the word of the Lord.

Then that closing scene of anguish. Abraham grasped the knife firmly and, lifting it up over Isaac's chest, he looks down on the face of the one who means more than life to him. Isaac in turn looks up, sees the knife reflecting the light of the sun, then shifts his gaze to his father's eyes. It is an agelong minute.

At that crucial moment came the dramatic break. Before the knife took its fatal plunge, Abraham hears a familiar voice calling his name twice. "Abraham. Abraham."

As he had at Beersheba, he answers, "Here I am."

The speaker is the Angel of the Lord, none other than God, the Son, in a pre-incarnate appearance. He says, in effect, "You don't have to touch your son. You have passed the test. Now I know that you fear me so much that you wouldn't withhold even your only son from me. Now I know that yours is a total commitment."

A Substitute Provided

Hearing a commotion in the bushes behind him, Abraham turns to see a ram trapped by its horns in the tangled briars. It all came to him in a flash. He would offer the ram to God in place of his son. The ram would die as a substitute. It would die that Isaac might be saved. God had provided a sacrificial victim in the nick of time. So Moriah got a new name that day: Jehovah Jireh, *The Lord Will Provide.* It was there that God provided a suitable offering.

Abraham must have quickly slashed the ropes that bound Isaac, and hugged him as he had never hugged him before. His tears must have flowed without restraint, tears of joy, tears of deliverance.

The Angel wasn't through with him, though. Because the patriarch had not withheld his only son from the Lord, the Angel swore that He would bless and multiply Abraham's descendants as the stars and the sand. They would triumph over their foes. Because Abraham had believed, all the nations of the earth would be blessed in his seed.

Abraham then returned south with Isaac to the young men who were waiting with the donkey, and the little group returned to Beersheba. What a conversation they must have had along the way. What a rehearsal of the Lord's wonderful providence, of the marvelous circumstance that the ram should be caught by its horns at that particular place and at that exact time! Surely it was more than chance. God had vindicated His promise. Isaac was spared.

Centuries later, another Father would ascend that hill with His Son. Only this time, He would not spare Him. This time the Son would die. He would die to put away our sins by the sacrifice of Himself.

Jehovah lifted up His rod
O Christ, it fell on Thee!
Thou wast sore stricken of Thy God;
There's not one stroke for me.
Thy blood beneath that rod has flowed:
Thy bruising healeth me.

For me, Lord Jesus, Thou hast died,
And I have died in Thee;
Thou'rt ris'n: my bands are all untied,
And now Thou liv'st in me.
The Father's face of radiant grace
Shines now in light on me.
        —Anne Ross Cousin

Sometimes total commitment means giving to God the dearest treasure of our heart.

10
The Burnt Offering

The Old Testament has two ceremonies or rituals that are object lessons designed to portray commitment to the Lord. One is the burnt offering, the other the vow of a Hebrew slave.

First, we see a faithful Hebrew approaching the Tabernacle to make a burnt offering to the Lord. As he leads a young bull with a rope halter, he is meditating on how good the Lord has been to him. The steadfast love of Jehovah, His mercy, and grace fill him with gratitude. With joy he comes to make a full surrender of himself as symbolized by a burnt offering. He remembers that the animal he offers must be clean, that is, it must chew the cud and have cloven hooves. It must also be without blemish. He is now going to offer it of his own free will.

Passing through the entrance of the curtained enclosure, he comes immediately to the brazen altar. He feels the heat radiating from it. Holding the rope in his left hand, he places his right hand on the animal's head. This ritual is full of meaning. He is saying, "This bullock is here in my place. I am identifying myself with it. What happens to it is what happens to me figuratively."

At this point he probably ties the legs of the bullock, front and aft, then rolls it over on its side. He takes a well-sharpened knife and, with a deft stroke, draws it across the bullock's throat. A priest catches the blood in a container and sprinkles it around the top of the altar. A few death spasms and the victim lies motionless.

The offerer skins the animal and cuts it in pieces. Then the priest lays the pieces on the altar.

A Total Sacrifice

It is now that the unique feature of the burnt offering appears. The individual parts of the dismembered body are burned on the altar until the whole carcass (except the skin) is consumed by fire.

This offering is a type of the Lord Jesus in His total consecration to the will of God. Totally immersed in the fires of God's judgment at Calvary, the fragrance of His sacrifice rose as a pleasant fragrance to the Father (Eph. 5:2). But to the offerer in the Old Testament and to believers today, it speaks of our presenting our bodies as a living sacrifice, holy, and acceptable to God, which is our reasonable service.

> *His Hands and Feet and Heart, all three*
> *Were pierced for me on Calvary,*
> *And here and now, to Him I bring*
> *My hands, feet, heart, an offering.*
> —Cecil J. Allen

An important feature of the burnt sacrifice is that it is a sweet savor offering. "The priest shall bring it all and burn it on the altar; it is a burnt sacrifice, an offering made by fire, a sweet aroma to the Lord" (Lev. 1:13b). When a Hebrew offered it to the Lord, he might have thought it was just a routine expression of thanksgiving. He might not have thought that he was doing anything extraordinary. But the fact is that the pleasing aroma reached the presence of the Lord.

So it is with believers today. When the Lord finds believers who are willing to present their bodies a living sacrifice to Him, He takes great pleasure in them. The Throne Room of the universe is filled with the fragrance of a sweet aroma. The lesson of the burnt offering is: "Give God all there is of you."

All for Jesus, all for Jesus!
All my being's ransomed pow'rs;
All my thoughts and words and doings,
All my days and all my hours.

Let my hands perform His bidding,
Let my feet run in His ways;
Let my eyes see Jesus only,
Let my lips speak forth His praise.

—Mary James

11
Earmarked for Life

Does it surprise you that there was slavery in Israel in Bible times? Well, there was. Sometimes it was the only way a bankrupt Israelite could extricate himself from a mountain of debt. The Bible records slavery as a fact of history without approving it as a social institution.

The Lord drew up laws that protected the rights of slaves and saved them from cruel and abusive treatment. One particular law decreed that a Hebrew slave had to be set free in the seventh year of his servitude. No matter how oppressive his conditions, he always had the hope of freedom. His master was obligated to supply the slave liberally with meat, wine, clothing, and the necessities of life when releasing him.

Sometimes, however, a bondservant realized that he was better off working for a kind, generous master than he would be if he were out on his own. So he didn't have to accept his freedom. He could express his commitment to his owner by a simple ritual. The master would take him to the door of the house, place an ear lobe against the door, and pierce it with an awl. The slave would say, "I love my master...I will not go away from you," and he would then become earmarked as a slave for life (Ex.21:2-6; Deut.15:11-18).

Some see a reference to the Lord Jesus in Psalm 40:6 as the One who committed Himself to permanent servitude. The words, "My ears Thou hast opened" are literally, "My ears You have dug." By this act He became indentured forever.

A Slave Forever

The application is clear. We were once the slaves of sin and of Satan: deceived, burdened, oppressed. The Devil was the worst of masters. Then we met Jesus. He saved us from our sins and from the dominion of the evil one. He has been good to us beyond imagination or calculation.

We can go out free, living for self, for pleasure, for material things, or we can choose to be His willing slaves. We can say, "I love my Master. I will not go out free." We can present ourselves to be His slaves forever. In the words of Handley Moule, we can sing:

> *My Master, lead me to Thy door;*
> *Pierce this now willing ear once more:*
> *Thy bonds are freedom; let me stay*
> *With Thee to toil, endure, obey.*
>
> *Yes, ear and hand, and thought and will,*
> *Use all in Thy dear slav'ry still!*
> *Self's weary liberties I cast*
> *Beneath Thy feet; there keep them fast.*
>
> *Tread them still down; and then I know,*
> *These hands shall with Thy gifts o'erflow;*
> *And pierced ears shall hear the tone*
> *Which tells them Thou and I are one.*

Frances Ridley Havergal captured the commitment of the Hebrew slave like this:

> *I love, I love my Master, I will not go out free,*
> *For He is my Redeemer, He paid the price for me.*
> *I would not leave His service, it is so sweet and blest;*
> *And in the weariest moments, He gives the truest rest.*
> *For He has met my longing with words of golden tone,*
> *That I shall serve forever—Himself, Himself, alone.*

In the Old Testament, there were hired servants and bondservants. The hired servants worked for wages. Money was their motivation. The bondservants belonged to their masters. At least some of them loved their masters—love was their motive. A bondservant like this was worth twice as much as a hired servant. When he was released at the end of six years, the master was instructed: "It shall not seem hard for you when you send him away free from you, for he has been worth a double hired servant in serving you six years" (Deut. 15:18). It is still the same today. Those who serve the Lord out of a heart of love are worth twice as much as those who "suppose that godliness is a means of gain" (1 Tim. 6:5).

12
Ruth and Esther

In the history of the pre-Christian era, there is no shortage of accounts of women who made history for God by their dedication. The culture of that time was demeaning to women, but many of them rose above that to show the world what true devotedness is. Two of them are honored in a special way by having a book of the Old Testament named after each of them.

Ruth

Ruth is a bright star in the galaxy of the committed ones. She had a fiercely loyal commitment to Naomi, her mother-in-law. But more than that, her life was surrendered to Naomi's God.

Naturally speaking, she was anonymous. She came from a family of nobodies, and from among the Moabites, a race that was cursed by God and despised by His people. She was a woman, and as such depreciated in that culture. Her husband died and left her childless. Her mother-in-law was a Jew, an alien, a foreigner in Ruth's homeland.

Then came that moment which the poet says comes to every man and nation, the moment to decide. In Ruth's case, the question was: Would she go with Naomi to Bethlehem-Judah or would she stay with her own people in Moab? Her mother-in-law tried to make it easy for her by suggesting that she remain at home. That is what her sister-in-law decided to do.

Noble Dedication

Ruth's decision was a classic of commitment:

Don't ask me to leave you and turn back. I will go wherever you go and live wherever you live. Your people will be my people, and your God will be my God. I will die where you die and will be buried there. May the Lord punish me severely if I allow anything but death to separate us (Ruth 1:16-17, NLT).

Her decision was emphatic. "Don't ask me to leave you. Don't even hint at it. Don't even think it. I have made up my mind to follow you. There's no turning back." To judge the extent of her devotedness, we note the following choices she made:

A new person to follow. "Don't ask me to leave you." Ruth detected something in Naomi that gave her confidence. This mother of Israel was worthy to be followed.

A new place to live. "Where you live, I will live." Suppressing her nationalistic spirit, her love for Moab, she was willing to make a break with family, friends, and native environment.

A new family. "Your people will be my people." She became a Jewish proselyte, a daughter of Abraham by adoption. She cast in her lot with God's people, despised by the world, yet the excellent of the earth.

A new religion. In the words, "Your God will be my God," Ruth said goodbye to the pagan gods, rituals, and shrines of Moab, and embraced the God of Abraham, Isaac, and Jacob.

A new place to die. When she said, "Where you die, I will die," she was signaling her intention to make her choice a lifelong commitment. She wanted to be identified with Naomi in her death, as well as in her life.

A new burial place. "[Where you are buried] I will be buried." Traditionally people wanted to be buried where their roots were. Jacob and Joseph both wanted their bodies transported from Egypt and buried in the Promised Land. It is quite natural. Even salmon have a homing instinct as their life comes to an end, but Ruth was determined not to have a trace of that.

An obscure young widow, she committed herself without reservation to the God of Israel. As a result, she met and married a man of outstanding character, became an ancestor of the Messiah, and, as we said, she has a book of the Bible named after her.

You never know on the day when you surrender entirely to the Saviour what treasures He has in store for you.

Esther

The other woman who gave her name to a Bible book is Esther. We probably would never have heard of her if she had waffled when faced with the issue of full surrender.

It was a marvelous converging of circumstances that caused a Persian king to choose her as his queen. The public thought it was her beauty. Wiser minds knew it was her God. The timing was perfect. She was in power when her cousin, Mordecai, exposed a plot against the king's life. She was in power when murderous Haman nearly succeeded in having Mordecai hanged and when that same villainous anti-Semite succeeded in having an unalterable decree passed to liquidate all Jews in the kingdom.

The spotlight was now on Esther. Would she go to the king and plead for the lives of her people (and herself, as well)? There were two problems. To approach the unpredictable monarch except when he held out his golden scepter was certain death. The likelihood of his showing grace at that particular time was diminished by the fact that he and Esther had not had marital relations for a month.

To strengthen her resolve, Mordecai sent word to her that if she didn't act, she wouldn't escape more than any of the other Jews. He was certain that God would somehow restore the Jews, but she would miss the blessing of being their deliverer. Then he topped his appeal with these undying words: "...who knows whether you have come to the kingdom for such a time as this!"

That was all Esther needed. She called on the Jews in the citadel to fast for three days. Then she promised to go to the king, adding, "...if I perish, I perish." She laid her life on the line.

That's commitment. If she hadn't made that decision, we wouldn't be reading about her right now. And it paid off. The king showed grace to her. She was able to expose Haman and his plot against her people. A new unchangeable decree was written, allowing the Jews to defend themselves. The enemies suffered crushing defeat, and Mordecai was promoted to be second to the king.

Commitment receives its greatest test in the fires of adversity.

13
And There Were Others

Caleb

You can doubtless think of still more examples of commitment in the Old Testament. Caleb certainly comes up for honorable mention. When he was eighty-five, he was still not satisfied with past exploits but wanted to chalk up new victories for the Lord. So he asked Joshua for permission to drive the Anakim out of Hebron. "Give me this mountain," are remarkable words for an eighty-five-year-old soldier who could have been fading away in quiet obscurity. His commitment is memorialized in these words: "He wholly followed the Lord God of Israel." What a tribute!

Jonathan

Jonathan was heir-apparent to the throne of Israel. Upon the death of his father, Saul he would be crowned king. But Jonathan loved David, and he had the spiritual discernment to know that David was marked out by God to be king. As a token that he relinquished his own right to the throne, he gave his robe to David. Later when they were together for the last time, Jonathan told David without mincing words, "You shall be king over Israel."

Concerning Jonathan's character, Merrill Unger writes:

His most remarkable characteristic was his ardent and unselfish devotion to his friends, which led him to give up his hopes of the throne, and even expose himself to death, for the sake of those he loved. Notwithstanding that his affection for his father was repelled by the latter, owing to the king's insanity, he cast his lot with his father's decline, and "in death they were not divided."[1]

The fact that Jonathan did not join David in exile should not be allowed to obscure his unusual large-heartedness, undivided allegiance, and unselfish commitment.

David's Faithful Followers

When David was king, he had some men who were fiercely devoted to him. One of them was Amasai, chief of the captains who came to him at Ziklag. We don't know much about him; in fact, he is mentioned in only one verse (1 Chron. 12:18). But he is memorable because of his eloquent pledge of commitment to the king:

We are yours, O David; we are on your side, O son of Jesse! Peace, peace to you and peace to your helpers! For your God helps you.

Ittai was another soldier who was sold out to the king. He was a Gentile, and you wouldn't ordinarily think of a Gentile being loyal to a Jewish monarch. But when David fled from Jerusalem as a result of Absalom's treason, the king tried to dissuade Ittai from going with him into exile. Ittai's outburst of loyalty to David is remarkable:

As the Lord lives, and as my lord the king lives, in whatever place my lord the king shall be, whether in death or life, even there also your servant will be (2 Sam. 15:21).

Then there were the three valiant soldiers who were with David in the cave of Adullam. At that time, the king was an outcast and an exile. One day, as he thought of his boyhood in Bethlehem and of how good the water from the well there had been, he breathed a sigh for a nostalgic drink of it. No water in the world was like it. When the three mighty men heard this, it was as if they snapped instantly to attention and said, "Your desire is our command, sir." In order to reach Bethlehem, they had to break through enemy lines, but they were indifferent to their own safety. They gladly placed themselves in harm's way. All that mattered was to please their leader. It was worth their lives just to get him a cup of that water.

David was so pleased when they returned with it that, rather than drink it, he poured it out to the Lord, saying, "Far be it from me, O Lord, that I should do this. Is this not the blood of the men who went in jeopardy of their lives?" (2 Sam. 23:17).

If David was so moved by the dedication of these men, how much more must "David's Greater Son" be when He finds that kind of commitment in His followers. Today our Lord Jesus thirsts for the souls of people in Europe, Africa, Asia, Australia, North and South America. When faithful missionaries and their supporters win the lost to Him, He sees the labor of His soul and is satisfied.

Uriah

Another man that must be mentioned is Uriah. Like Ittai, he was a Gentile and a soldier in David's army. It was with Uriah's wife, Bathsheba, that David committed adultery. When she became pregnant, the king feared public disgrace, so he called Uriah back from the battle front and in pretended generosity granted him rest and rehabilitation leave. He assumed that Uriah would have conjugal relations with his wife and would then be assumed to be the child's father. Uriah wasn't aware of the king's duplicity, but his faithfulness foiled David's plot to cover his sin. Listen to Uriah's dedication:

> The ark and Israel and Judah are dwelling in tents, and my lord Joab and the servants of my Lord are encamped in the open fields. Shall I then go to my house to eat and drink, and to lie with my wife? As you live, and as your soul lives, I will not do this thing (2 Sam. 11:11).

Thwarted in his plan, the king then stooped to what was probably the lowest point in his career. He gave instructions for Uriah to be placed in the thick of the battle against the Ammonites. Then the Israelites would withdraw, leaving the loyal soldier to certain death.

71

And that is what happened. It was despicable treachery. In this case at least, David was not worthy of the commitment of a man like Uriah. That can never be said of our Lord.

Daniel and His Three Friends

We must not forget Daniel and his three friends who lived with him as captives in Babylon. Because of their personal excellence, they had come to the attention of the king. He decided to melt them down, then recycle them as Chaldeans by changing their names, their language, their diet, their lifestyle, and their culture. Oh yes, and their religion. Their given Hebrew names all had the name of God in them: Daniel—God is my Judge; Hananiah—Jehovah is gracious; Mishael—Who is like God?; and Azariah—Jehovah is my Helper (or Keeper). Their new Babylonian names contained the names of pagan deities: Belteshazzar—Bel, the national god; Shadrach—perhaps the moon god or the city god; Meshach—means I am humbled (before my god); and Abednego—servant of Nebo.

The first real temptation to compromise came in the area of food and drink, which might seem quite harmless in itself. They were told to accept the royal menu (which was perhaps the best gourmet food and wine then in the world). By agreeing, they would enhance their prospects for advancement in the royal court. It would have seemed like ingratitude not to agree to the king's order after all he had done for them. They might have rationalized that they could eat the food without endorsing it in their hearts. Their fellow Jews outside the palace would never know. And besides, all the others were doing it.

But it was not kosher food; it might have been offered to idols, and to eat it would be violating the dietary laws which God had given to Israel. So "Daniel purposed in his heart that he would not defile himself with the portion of the king's delicacies, nor with the wine which he drank" (Dan. 1:8).

But before the incident could became a *cause célèbre,* Daniel wisely suggested an alternative. Let these young Hebrew fellows go on a vegetarian diet for ten days and see what happens. The steward agreed to the plan. Ten days later, the king found them to be more handsome, wiser, and having more understanding than all the others. He had to admit that they were ten times better than all his Babylonian magicians and astrologers.

By sticking to their principles in what might seem to others a trivial matter, they were honored by God and prepared for what would prove to be a more severe test.

The Furnace of Fire

Another test was not long in coming. The king of Babylon apparently developed an exaggerated idea of his own importance as a result of a dream, so he ordered a pillar to be erected. It was overlaid with gold and as tall as an eight-story building. It was his way of guaranteeing a unified religion as well as a unified government. On the day of its dedication, everyone was ordered to bow in worship. The penalty for refusal was to be cast into a burning fiery furnace.

Daniel seems to have been away at the time, but his example had not been wasted on his three friends. They took a resolute stand. Under no circumstances would they worship an idol.

Perhaps it was the court advisers who reported them, jealous that these captives should be set over the affairs of the Province of Babylon. When the king heard, he couldn't believe that anyone would dare to disobey his order. Did they think that their God could rescue them from his power? The young Hebrews knew that their God could. So when the king delivered his final ultimatum, they said:

> Our God whom we serve is able to deliver us from the burning fiery furnace, and He will deliver us from your hand, O king. But if not, let it be known to you, O king, that we do not serve your gods, nor will we worship the gold image which you have set up (Dan. 3:17-18).

They knew that it was better to burn than to compromise. Better to die than deny their principles. Better to go to heaven with a good conscience than stay on earth with a bad one.

The king was livid with rage. He ordered the furnace to be heated "to the max," and the three young non-conformists were thrown in. The thought of being consigned to such torture is enough to bring on cardiac arrest. But notice what happened.

The flames killed the executioners but not the Hebrews. The three young men were not deserted by the Lord. He was in the furnace with them. All the fire did was destroy the ropes that bound them. When they came out, their clothing was not burned, their bodies were not scorched, their hair was not singed, nor there was any smell of fire on them (Dan. 3:22-27).

The king made an edict honoring the God of the Jews and threatening death to anyone who spoke against Him. He also promoted the three fire-proof men.

Spurgeon said, "If you yield an inch, you are beaten; but if you will not yield—no, not the splitting of a hair—they will respect you. The man who can hide his principles, and conceal his beliefs, and so do a little wrong, is a nobody. You cannot shake the world if you let the world shake you."

The Den of Lions

By now Daniel was between eighty and ninety, a powerful figure in the kingdom of Persia. His jealous colleagues wanted a reason to get rid of him, but his spotless character and conduct made it difficult. In an unintended tribute to him, they concluded that the only way to get him was to outlaw prayer to Daniel's God.

So an unchangeable law was passed. In the next month anyone who prayed to any god or man except King Darius would be thrown to the lions.

Daniel could see no reason why he should stop praying, so three times a day he knelt in his room, facing toward Jerusalem, giving thanks, and making earnest supplication. That wasn't all. He knelt by an *open window,* just as he had always done. Why change now? Here was a man who preferred a den of lions to a day spent without prayer.

Since his colleagues were looking for Daniel to break the law, they didn't have long to wait. He didn't pray under the blanket in bed. He didn't pray silently—in his heart. No, he prayed aloud in full view. The reluctant king had no alternative; Daniel must become meat for the lions. And so he was thrown into the den.

But wait! Daniel was sleeping with the lions whereas the monarch was having a king-sized case of insomnia. In the morning, God's man came out in perfect condition. God had shut the lion's mouths. His accusers were slain, and his God was honored by a royal decree.

Think of the glory that came to God as a result of Daniel's commitment. That valiant man knew nothing of what Robert G. Lee called "invertebrate theology, jelly fish morality, seesaw religion, India rubber convictions, and somersault philosophy."

The committed ones we have been admiring had convictions for which they were willing to die. Their dedication to the Lord was final and irrevocable. For them the will of God was paramount. They had nothing but contempt for escape routes, for easy alternatives, for excuses. In life or in death, they were the Lord's.

ENDNOTE

1   *Unger's Bible Dictionary,* Chicago: Moody Press, 1967, p. 603.

14
Commitment in the New Testament

John the Baptist

Now we come to the New Testament to meet men and women who were dedicated to the Saviour to an unusual degree. There was John the Baptist. Our Lord commended him as a "burning and shining lamp," and "more than a prophet." John consistently spoke of his own unworthiness, determined that his Master would receive all the glory. He wasn't at all jealous when his disciples left him to learn at the feet of Jesus. His self-effacement and humility were exceeded only by his death-defying courage. Eventually Herod the Tetrarch ordered him to be beheaded.

The Apostles

There were the eleven apostles. When a younger John heard the Baptist cry, "Behold the Lamb of God," he began a life of untiring service, earning for himself the name, "the disciple whom Jesus loved." He did not die a martyr's death, like the others, but he lived a martyr's life. Simon Peter's commitment to Christ was undeniable, even if we tend to zero in on his weaknesses. To follow Christ, he abandoned his fishing trade on the best business day of his life (Luke 5:1-11). If the tradition is true, he asked to be crucified upside down, considering himself to be unworthy to die as His Master did. Details concerning some of the other apostles are sparse, but it is clear that they lost their hearts to the Lord, never to turn back.

Faithful Women

We must not forget the faithful women who ministered to the Saviour. There were those who anointed Him with costly perfume, washed His feet with their tears, and wiped them with their hair. There was the woman who cast "all that she had—her whole livelihood—into the treasury." In the house of Simon the leper, another prepared His body for burial. It was women who were last at the cross and first at the empty tomb. In the book of Acts and in the epistles we find Lydia, Priscilla, Lois, Eunice, and others.

Stephen

Stephen, a man full of faith, power, and the Holy Spirit, was the first martyr of the Christian church. He was preeminently a man of loyalty to Christ, choosing a violent death rather than compromise.

Paul

If Abraham is the outstanding example of commitment in the Old Testament, the apostle Paul holds that distinction in the New Testament (not counting the Lord Jesus, of course). Before his conversion to Christ, Paul was a rising star among the orthodox of Judaism. Proud of his racial and religious credentials, he zealously promoted his own faith and sought to silence any religion that seemed to be a threat.

On the road to Damascus, however, he met the glorified Lord, and in that moment he "heard a sweeter story! He found a truer gain" (Mary Bowley Peters). He became an ardent follower of the One he had been persecuting. A fire was set in his soul that would never go out. His question, "Lord, what wilt Thou have me to do?" was, first of all, an acknowledgment of Jesus as his Lord and Master. Then it was a total surrender of his will to the will of Christ, whatever that might entail. The rest of his life and his execution in Rome were the answer to his question.

Few people have ever run the gamut of human emotions and suffering as did Paul. He knew what sorrow was: perplexity, disappointment, heartbreak, betrayal. He was slandered by his foes and deserted by some of his friends. When some of the Corinthian believers were questioning the validity of his apostleship, he hurled out this unforgettable challenge:

Are they Hebrews? So am I. Are they Israelites? So am I. Are they the seed of Abraham? So am I. Are they ministers of Christ?—I speak as a fool—I am more: in labors more abundant, in stripes above measure, in prisons more frequently, in deaths often. From the Jews five times I received forty stripes minus one. Three times I was beaten with rods; once I was stoned; three times I was shipwrecked; a night and a day I have been in the deep; in journeys often, in perils of waters, in perils of robbers, in perils of my own countrymen, in perils of the Gentiles, in perils in the city, in perils in the wilderness, in perils in the sea, in perils among false brethren; in weariness and toil, in sleeplessness often, in hunger and thirst, in fastings often, in cold and nakedness—besides the other things, what comes upon me daily: my deep concern for all the churches. Who is weak, and I am not weak? Who is made to stumble, and I do not burn with indignation? (2 Cor. 11:22-29).

In another place he wrote:

...in all things we commend ourselves as ministers of God: in much patience, in tribulations, in needs, in distresses, in stripes, in imprisonments, in tumults, in labors, in sleeplessness, in fastings; by purity, by knowledge, by longsuffering, by kindness, by the Holy Spirit, by sincere love, by the word of truth, by the power of God, by the armor of righteousness on the right hand and on the left, by honor and dishonor, by evil report and good report; as deceivers, and yet true; as unknown, and yet well known; as dying, and behold we live; as chastened, and yet not killed; as sorrowful, yet always rejoicing; as poor, yet making many rich; as having nothing, and yet possessing all things (2 Cor. 6:4-10).

In his biography of Paul, James Stalker writes:

There was never such singleness of eye or wholeness of heart. There was never such superhuman and untiring energy. There was never such an accumulation of difficulties victoriously met and of sufferings cheerfully borne for any cause.[1]

Yet there was never a thought of giving up, or turning back. Having put his hand to the plow, he must endure. If this was the price of commitment to Christ, he would pay it—even to the pouring out of his life's blood. He had only one passion: it was Christ, and Christ alone.

Paul was not one of those brittle saints who faint at the sight of blood, or who say, "I would be a soldier if it weren't for those horrible guns." When the scaffolding seemed to be crashing around him in Asia, he did not hotfoot it back to Antioch with some whining excuse. He never gave up. He had never learned to sound retreat.

Listen to the magnificent response which he hurled out as he thought of his life of pain and persecution:

But none of these things move me; nor do I count my life dear to myself, so that I may finish my race with joy, and the ministry which I received from the Lord Jesus, to testify to the gospel of the grace of God (Acts 20:24).

It was no wild boast for him to say at the close of life, "I have fought the good fight, I have finished the race, I have kept the faith" (2 Tim. 4:7).

He lives among us today with a life a hundredfold more influential than that which throbbed in his brain while the earthly form that made him visible still lingered on the earth. Wherever the feet of those who publish the glad tidings go forth beautiful upon the mountains, he walks by their side as an inspirer and a guide; in ten thousand churches every [Lord's Day] and in a thousand thousand homes every day his eloquent lips still teach that gospel of which he was never ashamed; and wherever there are human souls searching for the white flower of holiness or climbing the difficult heights of self-denial, there he whose life was so pure, whose devotion to Christ was so entire, and whose pursuit of a single purpose was so unceasing, is welcomed as the best of friends.[2]

Martyrs

While still thinking of New Testament examples of commitment, we should not forget the many martyrs, known only to God, all who counted His "lovingkindness to be better than life." We should pay tribute to those, for instance, who died in the time of Nero. When fire consumed half the city of Rome, the Emperor blamed the Christians, though there is a strong suspicion that he was the guilty culprit. He ordered believers to be covered with tar and then ignited to provide illumination for his garden parties. Of these men and women who loved not their lives unto death, we can only say they were Christians "of whom the world was not worthy" (Heb. 11:38).

ENDNOTES

1   James Stalker, *The Life of St. Paul,* New York: Fleming H. Revell Co., 1912, p. 15.

2   Ibid., pp. 143-144.

Part III

COMMITMENT IN CHURCH HISTORY

15
Commitment in Later Church History

We must not think that all the dramatically dedicated saints lived in Bible times. The Lord always has a remnant of men and women who make a full surrender of their lives to Him.

We cannot forget the early Christian martyrs like Polycarp. When the proconsul threatened to burn him alive, Polycarp said, "The fire you threaten burns but an hour and is quenched after a little, but you do not know the fire of coming judgment, and everlasting punishment, that is laid up for the impious. But why do you delay? Come, do what you will." When the soldiers began to nail him to the stake, he said, "Leave me as I am. For He who grants me to endure the fire will enable me also to remain on the pyre unmoved, without the security you desire from nails."

There were the heroes of the catacombs. At that time, Caesar wanted to unify his empire, which had many diverse elements racially, culturally, and linguistically. So he introduced Caesar-worship. Every citizen was commanded under pain of death to take a pinch of incense, put it on a Roman altar once a year, and say "Caesar is Lord." They didn't have to believe it; all they had to do was say it. But these believers would not. Their invariable response was "Jesus is Lord." At the last minute they could recant their faith in Christ, place the incense on the altar, and say "Jesus be cursed." But they were faithful to the Saviour, and that allegiance cost them their lives.

The pages of history are stained with the blood of the Waldensians, Moravians, Huguenots, and Scottish Covenanters.

JOHN WYCLIFFE (1320-1384), known as the morning star of the Reformation, insisted on the right of the common people to have the Word of God in an understandable language. To that end he produced the first complete version of the English Bible. He taught that the Bible is the only authority in matters of faith and practice, and that the doctrine of transubstantiation is a blasphemous deceit. This, of course, brought him into conflict with the Roman church. Forty-four years after his death, his body was exhumed, burned to ashes, and thrown into the Swift River. If Wycliffe saw this from his heavenly vantage point, I think he must have laughed.

JOHN HUSS (1369-1415), was influenced by Wycliffe's teachings and propagated them in Bohemia. Because he fearlessly rebuked the vices of the clergy, he was hounded for years, then ex-communicated by the Pope. For preaching the gospel, he was finally burned at the stake by a church that is drunk with the blood of the saints.

WILLIAM TYNDALE (1494-1536), gave us the first printed version of the Bible in English. When his friends and others began to read the Word, the clergy became alarmed at this threat to their authority. Cardinal Wolsey defended the Church against the "pernicious heresy" of the Bible. When a supposedly learned clergyman was sent to convert Tyndale, the latter said, "If God spares my life, ere many years, I will take care that a plough-boy shall know more of the Scriptures than you do." He spent the last seventeen years of his life in captivity, then was strangled and burned.

COUNT ZINZENDORF (1700-1760), a leader of the Bohemian Brethren, stood before a picture of Christ crucified by Steinberg that contained the words, "All this I did for thee. What hast thou done for Me?" That searching question led him to consecrate his life, wealth, and talents to the cause of the Lord. He organized a company of Christian refugees on his lands in the village of Herrnhut, and it was from there that the modern Christian missionary movement began.

HUGH LATIMER (1485-1555), a great Protestant bishop, said, "If I see the blood of Christ with the eye of my soul, that is true faith." That concept, of course, was heresy to the established church. When both men were tied to the stakes, Latimer said to his fellow martyr, Nicholas Ridley, "Be of good cheer, Mister Ridley. By the grace of God we shall this day light such a candle in England as shall never be put out." And they did!

THOMAS CRANMER (1489-1556), in a moment of weakness, signed a recantation of his Scriptural position. But he recovered his courage and went to the stake, holding first into the flames the guilty hand that had signed the recantation and saying, "Perish this unworthy hand!"

THE TWO MARGARETS: Because of their loyalty to Christ and refusal to bow to pressures from the political establishment, **MARGARET MACLACHLAN** (1622?-1685) and **MARGARET WILSON** (1667-1685) were condemned to be drowned by the tide. The former was 63, the latter 18. Despite urgent and incessant appeals to them to submit to their foes, they steadfastly refused. So Margaret MacLachlan was tied to a stake in deep water. The other Margaret was tied to a stake farther inland. The authorities assumed that when Miss Wilson saw the older woman die, she would recant. As the tide was finally up to the chin of the senior martyr, the spectators could hear her saying: "For I am persuaded that neither death nor life, nor angels, nor principalities, nor powers, nor things present, nor things to come, nor height, nor depth, nor any other created thing, shall be able to separate us from the love of God..." Before she could finish, the water had covered her and she was delivered from the sadism of Christ's enemies.

When Margaret Wilson saw her die, she was not weakened in

her resolve. Instead she said, "If God can give grace to an older woman to die, He can give grace to me." And so it was. The tide came in, covered her, and she went home to heaven to see the King she loved more than life.

JOHN BROWN (? - 1685) was one of the Scottish Covenanters who would rather be dead than be disloyal to the Lord Jesus and to the principles of the Word of God. One day Graham of Claverhouse and his men closed in on John as he was working near his house and ordered him inside. Mrs. Brown was there with a baby in her arms. Claverhouse ordered his men to shoot, but they had heard John Brown pray a few minutes earlier, and they couldn't obey the order. So Claverhouse himself shot the godly Scot, then turned to Mrs. Brown and asked, "What do you think of your husband now?"

With John's body lying at her feet, she replied, "I always thought a great deal of him, but I never thought as much of him as I do now."

When Claverhouse said, "It would be justice to lay you beside him," she shot back, "If you were permitted, I doubt not that your cruelty would go that length, but how will you make answer for this morning's work?"

MARTIN LUTHER (1483-1546), was saved through reading Paul's letter to the Romans. He was outraged by the sale of indulgences to build Saint Peter's church in Rome. When placed on trial, he refused to bow to the final authority of the Pope, acknowledging only the direct Lordship of Christ. His commitment shone out in his memorable words, "My conscience is captive to the Word of God." He later championed the three solas of the Protestant Reformation: *sola fide* (faith alone); *sola gratia* (grace alone); *sola Scriptura* (the Bible alone). He translated the Bible into the German language, and contended valiantly for the faith.

Someone said of **JOHN CALVIN** (1509-1564), another reformer, "He was intense in the service of the Lord, to whom he had given his heart fully." Although he was not clear as to the spheres of authority between the Church and the civil government, his teaching that salvation is by faith apart *from* works but *unto* works made him one of the most outstanding figures of the Reformation era.

Likewise we remember **JOHN KNOX** (1513-1572), a fearless defender of the faith in Scotland. Strongly influenced by Calvin, he was a tireless foe of idolatry and of all the heresies and unbiblical teachings of the Pope. It was he who said, "Give me Scotland or I die." One biographer said of him, "Knox, a man of unyielding strength of character and a spiritual giant, molded the thought of an entire nation probably as no other man has ever done."[1] The Catholic Queen Mary said she feared his prayers more than all the armies of England.

It would take a multi-volume encyclopedia[2] to tell the stories of men and women in every century who have followed Christ, taken up the cross daily, and resisted every effort to make them deny their faith.

ENDNOTE

1 John W. Kennedy, *The Torch of the Testimony,* Beaumont, Texas: The Seed Sowers, 1965, p. 149.

2 Some helpful volumes that partially cover the period include:
   Foxe's Book of Martyrs, by John Foxe, various editions
   Miller's Church History, by Andrew Miller, Zondervan
   The Pilgrim Church, by E. H. Broadbent, out of print
   Fair Sunshine, by Jock Purves, Banner of Truth
   Martyrs Mirror, Thieleman J. van Braght, Herald Press

16
Commitment in Recent History

Now we come to the last century or two. Are the ranks of the committed getting thinner? Perhaps the pressures of modern life, the love of material things, and preoccupation with pleasure have caused many to forget their original vows and leave their first love. But the voice of the Holy Spirit still calls men and women to full surrender and, every once in a while, some respond.

Anthony Norris Groves (1795-1853)

Anthony Norris Groves was the first missionary from those known as Brethren. A wealthy dentist, he left luxury and prestige to preach the gospel in Baghdad, then India, putting into practice the principles of Christian devotedness. In so doing, he proved that it was possible to take the teachings of the Lord literally. He taught that life's great goal is the exaltation of Jesus, and that we should surrender all we have to achieve this worthy aim. The Christian's motto should be: "Labor hard, consume little, give much, and all to Christ." In his radical discipleship, he believed that laying up treasures on earth was as contrary to the Word of God as adultery. Who can deny it when the Bible forbids both?

John Nelson Darby (1800-1882)

John Nelson Darby, contemporary with Groves, had the same spirit of self-sacrifice. He tramped the Wicklow mountains of Ireland and saw hundreds of Roman Catholics won to Christ. He preached on the Continent for twenty-six years without unpacking his suitcase. Everywhere he went, New Testament assemblies were planted. He lived for days on milk and nuts. One day he sat in a cheap Italian boarding house and sang, "Jesus, I my cross have taken, all to leave and follow Thee." His travels took him to most of the English-speaking world. He translated the Bible into French, German, and English, and his own writings fill over thirty-four volumes. God used him to develop dispensational theology, and to revive the truth of the Rapture of the Church and of the priesthood of all believers. Dwight L. Moody and C. I. Scofield were greatly influenced by his teachings. Bible schools in the United States also felt the impact of his teaching. Few men since the apostle Paul have had such a wide-reaching ministry. His philosophy was, "Ah, the joy of having nothing, and being nothing, seeing nothing but a living Christ in glory, and being careful for nothing but His interests down here."

George Müller (1805-1898)

George Müller is best known for his orphanage in Bristol, England. It was operated by faith, without ever making its financial needs known. Müller's purpose was to show the people of Bristol that there is a God in heaven who answers prayer. One day Arthur Pierson asked him, "What is the secret of your great work and the wonderful things that God has done through you?"

Müller looked up for a moment, then bowed his head lower and lower until it was almost between his knees. He was silent a moment or two and then said, "Many years ago, there came a day in my life when George Müller died. As a young man, I had a great many ambitions, but there came a day when I died to all those things, and I said, 'Henceforth, Lord Jesus, not my will but Thine,' and from that day God began to work in and through me."

David Livingstone (1813-1873)

It is David Livingstone's commitment to Christ that accounts for his greatness. The world exalts him as an explorer and opponent of the slave trade, but it was his life for the Saviour that really counted.

His labors in Africa are high spots in the history of Christian missions. His wholehearted devotion to the Lord was expressed in his motto, "I will place no value on anything I have or possess except in relation to the kingdom of God."

When he was 59, he wrote, "My Jesus, My King, My Life, my All; I again dedicate my whole self to Thee." The word *furlough* was not in his vocabulary. He once wrote to a missionary society that he was ready to go anywhere—provided it was forward. One day his African brothers found him on his knees—dead. His heart was buried in Africa, and his body entombed in Westminster Abbey. The inscription there reads: "For thirty years his life was spent in an unwearied effort to evangelize."

Frances Ridley Havergal (1836-1879)

A biographer of Frances Havergal said of her: "She had none of the ordinary titles to fame. What singled her out was the note of absoluteness in her spiritual experience...In her consecration there was no limit and no reserve. She had learned the secret of abandonment, and she yielded herself utterly to God. By virtue of this, her writings reached and moved a multitude of souls with strange penetrating power."[1]

When she was twenty-one, she saw the painting of Christ, *Ecce Homo,* in the Art Gallery in Dusseldorf. She was so moved that she wrote her first hymn:

> *I gave My life for thee,*
> *My precious blood I shed,*
> *That thou might'st ransomed be,*
> *And quickened from the dead;*
> *I gave, I gave My life for thee,*
> *What hast thou given for Me?*
>
> *My Father's house of light,*
> *My glory circled throne,*
> *I left for earthly night,*
> *For wanderings sad and lone:*

I left, I left it all for thee,
Hast thou left aught for Me?

I suffered much for thee,
More than thy tongue can tell,
Of bitterest agony,
To rescue thee from hell;
I've borne, I've borne it all for thee,
What hast thou borne for Me?

And I have brought to thee,
Down from My home above,
Salvation full and free,
My pardon and My love;
I bring, I bring rich gifts to thee,
What hast thou brought to Me?

Seventeen years later, she summarized her autobiography in six verses, each of which described an actual experience in her life:

Take my life, and let it be
Consecrated, Lord, to Thee;
Take my moments and my days,
Let them flow in ceaseless praise.

Take my hands, and let them move
At the impulse of Thy love;
Take my feet, and let them be
Swift and beautiful for Thee.

Take my voice, and let me sing
Always, only, for my King;
Take my lips and let them be
Filled with messages from Thee.

Take my silver and my gold;
Not a mite would I withhold;
Take my intellect, and use
Ev'ry power as Thou shalt choose.

Take my will, and make it Thine:
It shall be no longer mine.
Take my heart; it is Thine own;
It shall be Thy royal throne.

Take my love; my God I pour
At Thy feet its treasure-store.
Take myself and I will be
Ever, only, all for Thee.

Hudson Taylor (1832-1905)

Hudson Taylor was the founder of the China Inland Mission (now the Overseas Missionary Fellowship). He was the person who opened inland China to the gospel. He identified with the Chinese people in dress, food, and in whatever other ways were possible. His work was carried on in faith; he believed that God pays for what He orders. There was no need for him to solicit funds. In this policy, he followed George Müller who, incidentally, contributed generously to Taylor's work.

Charles Haddon Spurgeon (1834-1892)

Charles Haddon Spurgeon, "the prince of preachers," was filling large auditoriums before he was twenty. His printed sermons still enjoy wide circulation, as well as his *Treasury of David* (on the Psalms) and his *Morning and Evening Readings*. Like so many of God's choice servants, he was plagued with illness and laid down his Bible for the last time in 1892.

C. T. Studd (1860-1931)

C. T. Studd was born into a wealthy English home. His father was saved under Moody's preaching, and C. T. trusted Christ a year later. In university, he was cricket champ and a member of the Cambridge Seven.

His life motto was, "If Jesus Christ be God and died for me, then no sacrifice can be too great for me to make for Him." That conviction led him to serve in China, India, and Africa. He was one of

"God's irregulars," the kind that gets most of the work done. He founded the World Evangelization Crusade. Rather than return home and retire, he chose to remain in Africa and die there.

Amy Carmichael (1867-1951)

Amy Carmichael devoted her life to serving among Indian girls who might otherwise have been temple prostitutes. Of Irish stock, she had tremendous strength of character and leadership ability. The measure of her devotion to Christ is best seen in her writings.

The vows of God are on me. I may not stay to play with shadows or pluck earthly flowers till I my work have done and rendered up an account.

And, in another place she wrote:

> *From prayer that asks that I may be*
> *Sheltered from winds that beat on Thee;*
> *From fearing when I should aspire,*
> *From faltering when I should climb higher,*
> *From silken self, O Captain, free,*
> *Thy soldier who would follow Thee.*
>
> *From subtle love of softening things,*
> *From easy choices, weakenings,*
> *Not thus are spirits fortified,*
> *Not this way went the Crucified.*
> *From all that dims Thy Calvary,*
> *O Lamb of God, deliver me.*
>
> *Give me the love that leads the way,*
> *The faith that nothing can dismay,*
> *The hope no disappointments tire,*
> *The passion that will burn as fire.*
> *Let me not sink to be a clod.*
> *Make me Thy fuel, Flame of God.*

William Borden (1887-1913)

William Borden, like C. T. Studd, forsook an environment of luxury and wealth to answer the call of Christ. His wholeheartedness for Christ can be summarized in the motto, "No reserve, no retreat, no regrets." He said, "In every man's heart there is a throne and a cross. If Christ is on the throne, self is on the cross; and if self, even a little bit, is on the throne, Jesus is on the cross in that man's heart. If Jesus is on the throne, you will go where He wants you to go. Jesus on the throne glorifies any work or place."

Eric Liddell (1902-1945)

Eric Liddell's commitment to the Lord included a steadfast commitment to the Lord's Day. In the 1924 Paris Olympics, he adamantly refused to compete in the 100 meter event (for which he had qualified) because it was scheduled to be held on a Sunday. Some called him a traitor to Scotland and to Britain. The British athletic authorities were horrified. But he was unmoved. Eventually, he agreed to run the 400 meter race, even though it wasn't his event, because it was on a weekday. Before the race, the man who gave Eric his rub-downs handed him a slip of paper with these words: "In the old book it says, 'He that honors Me I will honor.'" Liddell won the race and set a new world's record. Later, when he died as a missionary in a Japanese internment camp, a leading national newspaper said, "Scotland has lost a son who did her proud every day of his life."

Betty Scott Stam (1906-1934)

While still a student in Bible School, Betty Scott Stam wrote this covenant in the front of her Bible:

> Lord, I give up my own purposes and plans, all my own desires, hopes and ambitions (whether they be fleshly or soulish), and accept Thy will for my life. I give myself, my life, my all, utterly to Thee, to be Thine forever. I hand over to Thy keeping all of my friendships, my love.

All the people whom I love are to take second place in my heart. Fill me and seal me with Thy Holy Spirit. Work out Thy whole will in my life, at any cost, now and forever. "To me to live is Christ, and to die is gain" (Phil. 1:21).

She and her husband gave their lives utterly to Christ as missionaries to China. They were beheaded in 1934. Their story is told in *The Triumph of John and Betty Stam.*

Jim Elliot (1927-1956)

All who knew Jim knew that he was like the burning bush— burning but not consumed. My own lasting impression of him was his unbending intolerance of anything that stood between the heart's devotion and Christ. In this he agreed with James Denney, who wrote:

If God has really done something in Christ on which the salvation of the world depends, and if he has made it known, then it is a Christian duty to be intolerant of everything which ignores, denies, or explains it away.[2]

You feel this intolerance when you hear Jim praying:

He makes His ministers a flame of fire. Am I ignitible? God deliver me from the dread asbestos of "other things." Saturate me with the oil of the Spirit that I may be aflame. But flame is transient, often short-lived. Canst thou bear this, my soul—short life? In me there dwells the Spirit of the Great Short-Lived, whose zeal for God's house consumed Him...Make me Thy fuel, Flame of God.[3]

Jim's philosophy was, "He is no fool who gives what he cannot keep to gain what he cannot lose." Together with four other young men who were ablaze for God, he died of Auca spears beside an Ecuadorean river.

ENDNOTES

1 Thomas Herbert Darlow, *Francis Ridley Havergal: A Saint of God. A New Memoir,* London: Nisbet.

2 Further documentation unavailable.

3 Elisabeth Elliot, *Through Gates of Splendor,* N.Y.: Harper & Bros., 1957, p. 18.

Part IV

THE HIGH CALLING
OF COMMITMENT

17
Go for the Gold

While I was writing the previous chapter, the Summer Olympics were going on in Atlanta. The world was witnessing some superlative examples of commitment from an earthly standpoint.

Every four years athletes from about 197 countries gather for the Summer Games. Mostly young people, they are the best that these countries can send to compete in the various sports. As far as physical prowess and skill are concerned, they are world class. Countries don't waste their money on second-rate athletes. They want the best.

Preparation

How are these exceptional young people sorted out from the common herd? No doubt, they have natural ability in their sports. Their bodies were created with just the right coordination of mind and muscles. But that is not enough. Before coming to the Games, they have practiced almost interminably. For example, one swimmer is reported to have practiced ten hours a day, six days a week, for seventeen years. The U.S. women's synchronized swimming team practiced swimming six hours every day and did aerobic exercises every day for a full year. That kind of discipline is typical of the winners. Behind every gold, silver, or bronze medal are years of disciplined practice.

Motivation

These athletes have enormous motivation. They are going for the gold. They are forever looking forward to the time when they will appear before the judges and when the victor's medal will be draped around their neck. They dream of the fame that could come to them, and of the money they might receive from lucrative endorsement deals. They anticipate the tumultuous cheers of the crowd.

Their minds are focused. They do not waste their time on trivia. If they are gymnasts, they are dedicated to refining their routines. No pain or weariness is allowed to interfere with their goal. Many of the normal relationships of life have to take second place. One thing and only one thing occupies their minds—that gold medal.

They have disciplined their bodies and brought them into subjection. They could have "pigged out" with favorite foods and drinks, but they knew that if they did, they couldn't win. They realized that they had to be temperate in all things.

Every sport has its own language, and the athletes master that language. They add new words to their vocabulary. They consider it a small price to pay.

Then come the eliminations. One by one the aspirants are dropped until the best person or team has proved itself.

Competition

Finally the Olympic games arrive. This is the moment of a lifetime, the goal toward which the athletes have striven, worked, practiced, dreamed. As they come front and center, we notice the determined look on their faces. No silly, sickly smiles. They are going to give it all they have.

Every nerve is stretched. Every muscle is tense. They're off! With all the determination of which they are capable, they give it their best.

Of course, they must observe the rules of the contest. Any deviation will result in a loss of points, and could cost them the prize. They divest themselves of everything unnecessary. This is not the time to wear attention-getting clothing or burden themselves with accessories that would add to their weight load.

Many of the sports require enormous endurance. Those bodies

take a terrible pummeling. But there is no holding back. No pain, no gain. No price is too great to pay. Oceans of emotions flow. Often those who fail to win break down in anguished sobbing. It seems that years of preparation have gone down the drain in a moment of time. For some, hopefully, there may be another chance.

One young gymnast performed her final vault in the team competition with a sprained ankle. She did it voluntarily. And it was worth it when she won the gold medal for her team.

The winners experience a moment of exhilaration when they stand as their national anthem is played. They walk away with their medal, the coveted prize.

Christians who watch the games cannot help seeing spiritual applications. The similarities and contrasts are striking.

God is looking for the best contestants. In His case, however, the best are not the ones that the world would choose. They may be the ones whom the world considers foolish, weak, base, despised—the nobodies (1 Cor. 1:27-28). The ones who are the best for God are the ones who give Him their best, who consider Him worthy of all they have and are.

Youth is God's best time with the soul. It is when the metal is still molten and can still be shaped. It is the time when energy is high and when mental faculties are sharpest.

Christians, too, must practice. God calls us to the practice of holiness. "He does not delight in the strength of the horse; He takes no pleasure in the legs of a man. The Lord takes pleasure in those who fear Him, those who hope in His mercy" (Ps. 147:10). Our practice is not physical; it is spiritual. For the believer, "…bodily exercise profits a little, but godliness is profitable for all things, having promise of the life that now is and of that which is to come" (1 Tim. 4:8). This means shutting ourselves off from the noise pollution of the world to spend time in the Word, in prayer, in meditation, and in study. It means a life of consistent obedience to the Word.

Paul was probably thinking of the original Olympic Games when he wrote: "Do you not know that those who run in a race all run, but one receives the prize? Run in such a way that you may obtain

105

it....Therefore, I run thus: not with uncertainty. Thus I fight; not as one who beats the air. But I discipline my body and bring it into subjection, lest, when I have preached to others, I myself should become disqualified" (1 Cor. 9:24-27).

Notice that Paul did not run with uncertainty. He was focused. He kept the goal in view and ran straight for it. He did not beat the air, wasting time and effort with ineffective blows. He tried to make every movement count for the kingdom. He disciplined his body and brought it into subjection. He could have catered to the flesh, satisfying its whims and appetites, but had he done so, he never could have been victorious in the Christian life. He dreaded defeat. After having called others to the games, he feared being disqualified himself.

Our minds should be focused. We should look to Jesus, the Author and Finisher of our faith (Heb. 12:2). Constantly, we should guard against distractions. Spurgeon said, "He who has seen Jesus die will never go into the toy business. A child, a pipe, a little soap, and many pretty bubbles. The cross alone can wean us from such play."

We must be willing to learn a new language, the language of heaven. We must add new words to our vocabulary, words like justification, sanctification, propitiation, and glorification. In time, we might be required to learn a foreign language in order to serve in a different country.

Eliminations

Then come the eliminations. The fallout in the Christian Olympics is sobering. Dr. Paul Beck said to his prospective son-in-law: "John, as you get ready to enter the ministry, I want to give you some advice. Stay true to Jesus! Make sure that you keep your heart close to Jesus every day. It's a long way from here to where you're going to go, and Satan's in no hurry to get you. It has been my observation that just one out of ten who start out in full-time service for the Lord at twenty-one are still on track by the age of sixty-five. They're shot down morally, they're shot down with discouragement, they're shot down with liberal theology; they get obsessed with making money...but for one reason or another, nine out of ten fall out."[1]

John went home and in the front of his Scofield Bible, he wrote the names of twenty-four of his peers and contemporaries who were dedicated to Jesus Christ, committed to full-time work for the Lord. Thirty-three years later, only three names remained of the original twenty-four.

Howard Hendricks conducted a survey of 246 men in full-time ministry who experienced personal moral failure within a two-year period. That's roughly ten a month for two years. Each of them started strong. Over eighty percent of them became sexually involved with another woman as a result of counseling the woman. Each of the 246 was no doubt convinced that "it could never happen to me."

In the Christian race, we must divest ourselves of everything unnecessary. That is what the writer to the Hebrews means: "...let us lay aside every weight, and the sin that so easily ensnares us" (Heb. 12:1b). No excess baggage. We must not get entangled in the affairs of this life (2 Tim. 2:4).

Christ must be first in our life. That is why Paul writes so forcefully: "But this I say, brethren, the time is short, so that from now on even those who have wives should be as though they had none,[2] those who weep as though they did not weep, those who rejoice as though they did not rejoice, those who buy as though they did not possess, and those who use this world as not misusing it. For the form of this world is passing away" (1 Cor. 7:29-31).

We will experience plenty of emotions. There are tears for a perishing world and for the low spiritual condition of the Church. There are tears for our own failures and shortcomings. We weep when promising disciples backslide. And there is joy for every triumph of the gospel, for every believer who goes on faithfully for the Lord, and for every answer to prayer.

The Judge sits on the *Bema,* that is, the Judgment Seat. He has no gold medals in His hand. Just crowns. Crowns of life. Crowns of glory. Crowns of righteousness. These are the incorruptible rewards.

And there is no pride of life at this time. No vaunting of self. As He places His nail-scarred hand on the shoulder of the victor, there is only one thing to do. Kneel before Him and cast the crowns at His feet. Christ alone is worthy!

What would happen if Christians showed the same zeal, motivations, discipline, and determination as the Olympians? What would happen if our young people spent as much time in the Word, in prayer, and in service for the Lord as the world's best athletes spend in practice?

The world would be evangelized.

ENDNOTE

1   Steve Farrar, *Finishing Strong, Sisters,* Oregon: Multnomah Books, 1995, p. 6.

2   Of course Paul is not suggesting that marriage partners neglect their mates. But Christ deserves our supreme loyalty, far above any human tie (*ed.*).

18
Commitment is Costly

It is a fact of life that commitment is necessary for anyone who wants to achieve excellence. Olympic athletes aren't the only ones who have to practice endlessly, train rigorously, and discipline themselves faithfully. People in every field of endeavor must be motivated to give their best and endure patiently. The medals and ribbons are not for couch potatoes or wanna-bees with slow blood.

> *The heights by great men reached and kept*
> *Were not attained by sudden flight,*
> *But they, while their companions slept,*
> *Were toiling upward in the night.*
> —Henry Wadsworth Longfellow

It Looks So Easy

We watch musicians in concert and admire their flawless performances. They play or sing with such finesse that it seems easy to us. Easy? What we don't realize is the years of focused practice it took for them to acquire this skill. Somebody once asked Paderewski, the famous pianist, what was the secret of his success. He replied, "Practicing scales hour after hour, day after day, till these poor fingers were nearly worn to the bone." Yet he was willing to do it in order to achieve fame as a pianist.

I often think of John James Audubon, the great artist and naturalist. He would rise at midnight and go into the swamps, night after night, to study the habits of certain night hawks. He considered

109

himself rewarded if, after crouching motionless for hours in the dark and fog, he gained one new fact about a single bird. One summer he went to the swamps near New Orleans to observe a shy waterfowl. It meant standing up to his neck in stagnant water while poisonous moccasin snakes swam past his face and great alligators passed and repassed his silent watch. "It was not pleasant," he said, his face glowing with enthusiasm, "but what of that? I have the picture of the bird." He would do that for the picture of a bird.

Famous writers tell how they achieved excellence. Edward Gibbon spent 26 years writing *The Decline and Fall of the Roman Empire.* John Milton habitually rose at 4 A.M. to work on *Paradise Lost.* Thomas Gray began his *Elegy in a Country Churchyard* in 1742 but didn't finish till June 1750. Ernest Hemingway said that he began every day reading and editing everything he had written to the point where he left off. "That way I go through a book several hundred times, honing it until it gets an edge like a bull-fighter's sword. I rewrote the ending of *A Farewell to Arms* 39 times on manuscript and worked it over 30 times in proof, trying to get it right." These men were willing to give such energy, zeal, and dedication to what they considered a worthy cause.

Think of the sacrifices that many business and professional people make. Extended stays away from family. The inconveniences of travel. Adjustment to jet lag. Lonesomeness of hotel rooms. Foreign languages. Weather extremes and strange foods. They are willing to do this for the dollar.

Blood, Sweat, and Tears

Commitment is the stuff of which explorers are made. Ernest Shackleton of Antarctic fame placed this ad in a London paper:

Men wanted for hazardous journey. Small wages. Bitter cold. Long months of complete darkness. Safe return doubtful. Honor and recognition in case of success.

Military commanders don't want chocolate soldiers who faint at the first sight of blood. Standing on the steps of St. Peter's in Rome,

Garibaldi said to the men gathered around him, "I offer you neither pay nor provision. I offer you hunger, thirst, forced marches, battles and death. Let him who loves his country with his heart and not only with his lips follow me." Dare we offer less to the Lord Jesus?

When a golfer asked Babe Didrickson Zaharias how to perfect his shot, she laughed. "Simple," she said. "First you hit a thousand golf balls. You hit them until your hands bleed and you can't hit any more. The next day you start all over again, and the next day and the next. And, maybe a year later, you might be ready to play 18 holes. After that, you play every day until the time finally arrives when you know what you are doing when you hit the ball."

It takes plenty of dedication for actors and actresses to memorize their lines, then rehearse until every movement and inflection are just right. Archeologists endure the broiling sun for weeks in search of a few potsherds. Those engaged in research forget the clock and the calendar as they press on for some new scientific breakthrough. And the list goes on.

What About Us

All this raises disturbing problems for those of us who are followers of the Christ of Calvary. We have the greatest Captain to follow. We have the greatest message to proclaim. And the greatest cause for which to live and die. If men and women will burn themselves out for recognition, honor, financial remuneration, love of country, and success, how much more should we be willing to give Him our all?

In his book *Dedication and Leadership,*[1] Douglas Hyde contrasted Communists and Christians:

> To the Christian there is an element of sheer tragedy in this—that people with such potentialities should give so much energy, zeal, and dedication to such a cause, while those who believe they have the best cause on earth often give so little to it. And their leaders are so often afraid to ask for more than the merest minimum.

The Christian may say that the Communists have the worst creed on earth. But what they have to appreciate is that the Communists shout it from the house-tops, while too often those who believe they have the best, speak with a muted voice when they speak at all.

An article in *Harvester Magazine* pointed out the same inconsistency:

Many of us who profess to love the Lord Jesus Christ and desire to serve Him are put to shame when compared to [dedicated people of the world]. So many acts of service in Christian work are done in a half-hearted way. They are fulfilled as tasks to be done, but there seems to be little effort in preparation or joy in the doing of them. A Sunday School teacher "gets by" with but a few minutes of study and less prayer, and then wonders why there is little fruit. A preacher "digs into the barrel" for an old sermon, thinking that it will do for the next Sunday, since few of the congregation will remember it in any event, and is puzzled that his audience is not stirred. Most of us fail to pray as we ought, for praying is hard work, and then we profess perplexity that we do not see answers to our prayers. Spiritual laziness is responsible for much spiritual barrenness.[2]

Endnotes

1 Douglas Hyde, *Dedication and Leadership,* Notre Dame, IN: University of Notre Dame Press, 1966, p. 32.

2 *The Harvester,* March 1957, p. 47.

19
God Wants the Best

A golden thread runs through the Scriptures, a truth that constantly reappears in the weaving of the Word. The truth is this: God wants the first and God wants the best. He wants first place in our lives and He wants the best we have to offer.

Flawless

When the Lord instituted the Passover, He instructed the Israelites to bring a lamb without blemish (Ex. 12:5). They were never to sacrifice to Him any animal that was lame, blind, defective, or flawed (Deut. 15:21; 17:1). That would be detestable.

Now it should be clear that God does not need any animals that man can offer to Him. Every beast of the forest is His, and the cattle on a thousand hills (Ps. 50:10). Why then did He legislate that only perfect animals should be sacrificed to Him? He did it for our good, not for His own. He did it as an object lesson to teach His people at least one fundamental truth: they can find joy, satisfaction, and fulfillment only by giving Him the proper place in their lives.

Firstborn

In Exodus 13:2, God commanded His people to set apart their firstborn sons and firstborn animals for Him: "Consecrate to Me every firstborn male. The first offspring of every womb among the Israelites belongs to Me, whether man or animal" (NIV).

The firstborn stands for that which is superlative and most highly esteemed. Thus Jacob spoke of Reuben, his firstborn, as "my might and the beginning of my strength, the excellency of dignity and the excellency of power" (Gen. 49:3). The Lord Jesus is spoken of as "the firstborn over all creation" (Col. 1:15) in the sense that He is the most excellent and that He holds the position of highest honor over all creation. In telling His people to sanctify their firstborn sons to Him, God was touching a sensitive nerve because in a patriarchal culture the oldest son had a special place of affection in his parents' hearts. It was all designed to teach them to say, in effect:

> *The dearest object I have known,*
> *Whate'er that object be,*
> *Help me to tear it from the throne,*
> *And worship only Thee.* —William Cowper

Firstfruits

Next God instructed the farmers to bring the firstfruits of the land to the house of the Lord (Ex. 23:19). When the grain crop began to ripen, the farmer was to go out to the field, reap an armful of the first ripe grain, and present it as an offering to the Lord. This sheaf of firstfruits acknowledged God as the Giver of the harvest, and pledged that He would receive His portion of it. Again, it is obvious that God didn't need the grain, but the people needed a constant reminder that the Lord was worthy of the first and best.

When sacrificial animals were cut up, the priests were sometimes allowed to take certain parts, the offerers were permitted to eat other parts, but the fat was always offered to the Lord (Lev. 3:16). The fat was considered to be the richest and best part of the animal, and therefore belonged to Him. Nothing but the best was good enough.

Some of God's kindly laws were also designed to safeguard the health of His people. Here, for instance, the prohibition against eating the fat might protect the people from arteriosclerosis, thought to be caused by excessive cholesterol. But the basic intent of this law was to teach the people to give the best to God.

First Dough

This obligation of putting God first extended to every area of life, not only to the place of worship but to the kitchen as well. The Lord's people were instructed to offer a cake of the first of their dough for a heave offering: "Of the first of your ground meal you shall give to the Lord a heave offering throughout your generations" (Num.15:21). Mixing a batch of dough seems like a mundane task, one that is not especially spiritual. But in offering the first of the dough to the Lord, a godly Jew was confessing that God must have first place in all of life. It was also a denial of any distinction between the secular and the sacred. While it was evident that God didn't need the dough, the Lord must be acknowledged as the Giver of the person's daily bread.

We see this principle laid on the line in an instruction to the Levites: "You must present as the Lord's portion the best and holiest part of everything given to you" (Num. 18:29, NIV). Since all of us become like what we worship, it is imperative that we entertain a proper appreciation of God. Low thoughts of God are destructive. Only when we creatures give the Creator the place He deserves will we rise above flesh and blood and attain the dignity for which we were designed.

As we follow this golden thread through the Old Testament, we see the lesson acted out when Elijah met a destitute widow in a place called Zarephath (1 Kings 17:7-24). He asked the woman for a drink of water and a piece of bread. She apologized that all she had was a handful of flour and a little oil, just enough to make one last meal for her son and herself before they died of starvation.

"Not to worry," said the prophet, "first make a little bread for me, then use the rest for yourself and the boy."

Now that sounds like a shockingly selfish request, doesn't it? It seems as though the prophet were guilty of bad manners. To say "Serve me first" is both callous and a breach of etiquette.

But what we must understand is that Elijah was God's representative. He was standing there in the place of God. He was not guilty of selfishness or rudeness. What he was saying was, "Look, I am God's prophet. In serving me first, you are really giving God first place, and as long as you do that, you will never lack the necessities of life. Your flour barrel will never go empty and your olive oil jug will never run dry." And that's exactly the way it turned out.

Solomon reinforced God's prior claim on our lives in the familiar words, "Honor the Lord with your possessions, and with the firstfruits of all your increase" (Prov. 3:9). That means that every time we get a raise in pay, we should be sure that the Lord is the first to get His portion.

First, the Kingdom

Coming over to the New Testament, we hear the Lord Jesus insisting that God must have first place: "But seek ye first the kingdom of God, and His righteousness; and all these things shall be added unto you" (Mt. 6:33). It is the same truth that Elijah shared with the widow: those who give the Lord the place of supremacy in their lives will never have to worry about the basic necessities of life.

Perhaps we become so familiar with the Lord's Prayer (Mt. 6:9-13) that we miss the significance of the order contained in it. It teaches us to put God first ("Our Father which art in heaven, hallowed be Thy name") and His interests ("Thy kingdom come, Thy will be done in earth, as it is in heaven.") Only then, and not before, are we invited to bring our personal petitions ("Give us this day our daily bread," etc.)

Just as God the Father must be given the place of supremacy, so must the Lord Jesus, as a Member of the Godhead. Thus we read, "...so that He Himself might come to have first place in everything" (Colossians 1:18, NASB)

The Saviour insisted that His people's love for Him must be so great that all other loves are hatred by comparison. "If any man come to Me, and hate not his father, and mother, and wife, and children, and brethren, and sisters, yea, and his own life also, he cannot be My disciple" (Luke 14:26, KJV). Jesus must be first in our love.

Faulty Offerings

Now, regrettably, the Lord does not always get the first and best

116

from His people. In Malachi's day, when it was time to make an offering to God, a farmer kept the best animals for breeding or sale, and gave the Lord the castoffs. He was saying that anything is good enough for the Lord. Profit in the marketplace came first. That's why Malachi thundered, "When you bring blind animals for sacrifice, is that not wrong? When you sacrifice crippled or diseased animals, is that not wrong? Try offering them to your governor! Would he be pleased with you? Would he accept you?" (Mal. 1:8, NIV).

A Christian mother was working feverishly in the kitchen while a preacher was visiting with her son in the living room. The preacher was holding forth on the wonderful opportunities in the work of the Lord for this young man's skills. Then a strident voice came from the kitchen, "Don't talk like that to my son. That isn't what I've planned for him."

One evening a Christian business executive was setting forth his goals for his son: an Ivy-league college, a prestigious career in business, and a comfortable retirement. The son wasn't interested. He wanted to spend his life in the Lord's service. They talked on into the night but were getting nowhere. Finally, the son said, "Well, Dad, do you want me to go on for the Lord or don't you?" The father later said to me, "That was the end of all argument."

On a happier note, Spurgeon said to his son. "My son, if God should call you to the mission field, I should not like to see you drivel down into a king."

What About Us?

What about today? How can we give the Lord the first and the best? How can we make this principle practical in our own lives?

We can do it in our employment by obeying those who are over us; by working heartily as for the Lord, not for men; by realizing that it is the Lord Christ whom we serve (Col. 3:22-24). If the demands of work begin to claim priority over the claims of Christ, we must be prepared to say to them, in effect, "Thus far you shall come, but no farther, and here shall your proud waves stop." We should be willing to do more for the Saviour than we would ever do for a corporation.

We can do it in our home by faithfully maintaining a family altar, during which we read the Bible and pray together. Yes, we can do it by raising children for the Lord, not for the world, for heaven and not for hell.

> *Give of thy sons to bear the message glorious;*
> *Give of thy wealth to speed them of their way;*
> *Pour out thy soul for them in prayer victorious;*
> *And all thou spendest Jesus will repay.*
> —Mary A. Thomson

We can do it in our local fellowship by faithful attendance and enthusiastic participation. George Mallone tells of an elder who turned down an invitation to a presidential dinner at the White House because his eldership responsibilities did not allow him to have that evening free.

After Michael Faraday had given a brilliant exposition on the nature and properties of the magnet, the audience proposed a formal vote of congratulation. But Faraday was not there to receive it. He had slipped away to the midweek prayer meeting at his church, a church that never had more than twenty members.

We can put God first in our stewardship of material things. We do this by adopting a simple lifestyle so that all the surplus can go into the Lord's work. We do it by sharing with those who have spiritual and physical needs. In short, we do it by investing for God and for eternity.

But the greatest way we can give God first place is by presenting our lives to Him, by committing ourselves to Him not only for salvation but for service as well. Nothing less than that is enough, when we think of all He did for us.

> *O Christ, Thy bleeding hands and feet,*
> *Thy sacrifice for me:*
> *Each wound, each tear demands my life*
> *A sacrifice for Thee.* —J. Sidlow Baxter

20
What Hinders Our Commitment?

The logic of commitment is inescapable. Think again of what God incarnate did on the cross.

- He died as a Substitute for you and for me.
- He put away sin by the sacrifice of Himself.
- God the Father placed our sins upon His divine Son and He paid the penalty.
- He shed His blood to buy us back from the sin market.
- It is impossible to overemphasize the fact that it was God incarnate who died there for us so that we might spend eternity with Him in heaven.

The death of our Creator on Calvary is unique. Nothing like it ever happened before, or ever will be repeated. That He would be willing to die for sinful creatures strains the imagination. It is too daring an idea for human beings to invent, too awesome for the human mind to take in. It was love beyond measure, grace beyond parallel, sacrifice without limit.

Inanimate creation responded to the magnitude of what was happening. Darkness shrouded the land. Rocks disintegrated. The earth shook. Tombs sprang open. The temple veil ripped from top to bottom. Only one human being, in a burst of insight, expressed the wonder of it all. He was the Roman centurion who said, "Truly this was the Son of God."

Compared to Calvary, all other events pale into insignificance.

119

All other deaths were trivial. All other hours were irrelevant. And it was all for you and for me.

Our Reasonable Response

To that logic, there is only one proper response:

> *O Jesus, Lord and Master,*
> *I give myself to Thee;*
> *For Thou, in Thy atonement,*
> *Did'st give Thyself for me.*
> *I own no other Master,*
> *My heart shall be Thy throne.*
> *My life I give, henceforth to live,*
> *O Christ, for Thee alone.*
> —Thomas O. Chisholm

Why doesn't every Christian make a complete consecration of his or her life to the Christ? To put it bluntly, it's because we don't think straight. Our minds are skewed by fears and falsehoods. Let us expose some of them to the light.

Fear of God's Will

We fear what God may ask of us. A surprising number of Christians assume that if they say, "Take my life," God will automatically respond, "Go to the mission field." To them, the will of God is synonymous with overseas missionary work. They think that it is the only calling the Lord has for dedicated disciples. In their minds, it conjures up visions of snakes, swamps, scorpions, spiders, suffocating humidity. It is the most formidable life imaginable.

Such a fear betrays a shallow and dishonoring view of the resourcefulness of our Lord. Far from being limited to one option, He has an infinite variety of plans for yielded people. He is a God of limitless creativity or as someone has said, "wondrous imagination." He "delights us with His incredible variety."

This fear also overlooks the fact that God is not in the business of dragging reluctant draftees. His soldiers are volunteers. Paul reminds us in Philippians 2:13 that He works in us both to will and to do for His good pleasure. In other words, He first puts the desire in our hearts, then gives us the ability to carry it out. This means that when a man or woman walks in the will of God, he is doing the thing he most wants to do. For him, it is the fulfillment of a dream.

Fear of What God Will Take

Some of us fear that God will rob us of something we treasure. When will we learn that He doesn't come to steal, kill, or destroy? He does not come as a Robber but as a Giver (Jas. 1:17). He comes to give abundantly. He does not withhold any good thing from those who walk uprightly (Ps. 84:11).

He takes only those things that would be detrimental to our temporal and eternal well-being. For instance, He frees us from the guilt, penalty, and power of sin. He delivers us from this present evil world and from the wrath to come. For these blessed subtractions we should be eternally grateful.

It doesn't make sense to be afraid of the will of God. His will is always "good, acceptable, and perfect." To be afraid of it is to be afraid of a blessing.

Fear of God's Denials

We also fear that the Lord may deny us something good. For many young people, marriage tops the list. Yes, they say they want the will of God, but there is a string attached. First they want to be sure of a mate. First the marriage altar, and only then the altar of sacrifice.

To cherish that reservation isn't total commitment. It means that God's will must be subject to my will in at least this one area. The living sacrifice is incomplete.

Actually, marriage is God's will for most of the human race. This is clear from the fact that most of us come from a long line of married people. But to make marriage a condition for full commitment is wrong. Bargaining with God shows that a person's will is not subjected to His. And it is playing with dynamite. The obsession

121

for a husband can become so strong that a young woman will plunge ahead into a marriage that could chain her from ever achieving God's perfect will. The Lord will grant her desire but will send leanness to her soul (Ps. 106:15). That is true of young men also, who look first of all for outward beauty rather than for spiritual character in a potential wife

If God should call to a life of singleness, He will give not only grace, but contentment as well. It enables Christians to give themselves to the service of Christ without distraction. It grants mobility that they would not otherwise have. It frees them from many of the cares of this life. Singleness is better than marital misery.

For most people, singleness will not be God's choice. But the final decision should be left to Him. His will is what matters. Why stubbornly choose a spouse outside God's will when He would very likely have given a better one of His choice anyway? "Those who want to get married in the worst possible way usually do just that."

Fear of Loss of Independence

There is also the fear that God's will might conflict with our plans for a career, a home in suburbia, a car or two loaded with all the latest gimmicks. Too often, what we really want is to give our best years to making a living, then give our retirement years to the Lord. Frankly, He doesn't want them. He doesn't want the burnt out end of a wasted life. Can you blame Him?

Fear of the Unknown

Some persons suffer from fear of the unknown. They don't have the faith of Abraham. When God called him, he stepped out, not knowing where he was going. He chose to walk in the dark with God rather than walk alone in the light.

Fear of Loss of Security

Others fear that following the Lord would mean a loss of financial security. "I might not have a visible means of support. I might have to depend on the gifts of others. I might have to be on welfare." We must learn that God is our only true security, and that He provides liberally for what He orders.

Fear of Hardships

There is the fear of loss of comforts. Our vivid imaginations race with pictures of outdoor toilets and only occasional showers—to say nothing of hand-me-down clothing, early Salvation Army furniture, and secondhand everything else, while our friends are living high off the hog, perhaps enjoying what actually turn out to be "the soft and effeminate luxuries that kill the soul."

Fear of Inadequacy

Some might humbly feel that they don't have any special gifts or talents to give to the Lord. They consider themselves inferior; yes, even worthless. But the saintly F. B. Meyer said:

I am only an ordinary man. I have no special gifts. I am no orator, no scholar, no profound thinker. If I have done anything for Christ and my generation, it is because I have given myself entirely to Christ Jesus, and then tried to do whatever He wanted me to do.

Our part is to give ourselves entirely to Christ. His part is to use us for His glory. If we can qualify as foolish, weak, base, despised nobodies, then we are in a good position to be used by Him (1 Cor. 1:26-28).

Fear of Loss of Status

Sometimes I think that the greatest hindrance to full dedication is pride. If we were honest, we would have to confess that we consider ourselves too big, too important for the kind of a life that we equate with Christian service. It's all right for others, but it's below our dignity. We covet a name for ourselves in the world. Anyone with that fatuous attitude should consider the following:

• We may climb the ladder of success, and then, when we have reached the top, find that the ladder has been leaning against the wrong wall.

• We may barter God's best for His second, third, fourth, fifth best.

• We may spend our life on things of no eternal consequences.

• We may end up with a saved soul and a lost life.

• We may go to heaven empty-handed.

Or all of the above.

21
Defective Commitment

Each of us knows something about faulty surrender. When we point the finger at Biblical examples, three fingers are pointing back at ourselves. When we are tempted to criticize Peter, and Ananias, and Sapphira, we cannot help but feel convicted. We see ourselves mirrored in their experiences.

Peter's Three Refusals

Despite his love and zeal for the Lord Jesus, Peter is somehow remembered for His three refusals. When the Saviour predicted His death and resurrection, "Peter took Him aside and began to rebuke Him, saying, 'Far be it from Thee, Lord; this shall not happen to Thee'" (Mt. 16:22, KJV). There is a lesson here. You don't call Jesus Lord and then contradict Him.

At another time, when the Master knelt before Peter to wash his feet, Peter protested, "Lord, dost Thou wash my feet?...Thou shalt never wash my feet" (John 13:6, 8). Notice the contradiction between the words *Lord* and *never*.

When Peter had the vision of a sheet descending from heaven with all kinds of creatures, the risen Christ said, "Rise, Peter; kill and eat." The apostle answered, "Not so, Lord!" (Acts 10:13-14). Anyone who answers like that must make a choice. It is either "Not so" or "Lord." It can't be both. We must either do what He says or stop calling Him Lord.

When W. Graham Scroggie was counseling a young woman who was in great soul-struggle over the matter of submission to Christ, he told the story of Peter at Joppa, how the Lord told him to rise and eat. Three times Peter said, "Not so, Lord." Scroggie said tenderly, "You can say 'Not so' and you can say 'Lord,' but you can't say, 'Not so, Lord.' I'm going to leave my Bible with you and this pen. You go into another room and cross out either the words 'Not so' or 'Lord.'"

The young woman was weeping softly when she returned. Scroggie looked at the Bible and saw the words *Not so* crossed out. She was saying "He's Lord. He's Lord." In telling the story later, Scroggie added, "Such is the stuff of holy obedience."

Hypocritical Surrender

Ananias and Sapphira were caught up in a mighty movement of the Holy Spirit. The early Christians were forsaking all to follow Christ. Ananias and his wife sold a piece of property and pretended to give all the proceeds to the Lord, but they kept back part of it for themselves. They professed complete consecration when it was not complete. They weren't the last ones to commit this sin. How often we sing, "All to Jesus I surrender," while our surrender is yet incomplete. If God struck down all who are guilty of defective commitment, the ranks of the church on earth would be noticeably thinned.[1]

Me First

In Luke 9:57-62, we have three other examples of faulty dedication. The first man called Jesus *Lord* and enthusiastically promised to follow Him anywhere. "Lord, I will follow You wherever You go." But when the Lord warned him that it might mean homelessness, he beat a hasty retreat. His "anywhere" became "not there."

The second man heard the call of Christ, "Follow Me," but he said, "Lord, let me first go and bury my father." There is no suggestion that his father was dying at the time. He might have been in the best of health. The would-be disciple wanted to stay at home until the uncertain time when the father would breathe his last. It might even happen that the father would outlive his son. That was defective commitment, giving a higher priority to something else rather than to the call of Christ. It was putting self before the Saviour; notice that the young man actually said, "me first." Then he as much as said, "not now" but "later." What kind of surrender is that?

The third man also called Jesus *Lord* and professed full dedication. "Lord, I will follow Thee..." But he spoiled it all by saying "but" and then adding "me first." "...but let me first go and bid them farewell who are at my house." He didn't mean a quick goodbye. Farewells at that time could extend into days of food and fellowship. He too put a condition to his commitment. Social conventions had a higher priority than lordship. Jesus is Lord, but...

Years ago, this prayer appeared in the *Daily Notes* of the Scripture Union. It is still apropos:

Forgive us, O Lord, for so often finding ways of avoiding the pain and sacrifice of discipleship. Strengthen us this day to walk with Thee no matter what the cost may be. In Thy Name, Amen.

ENDNOTE

1 As noted earlier, even if we can't sing, "All to Jesus I surrender" as our present experience, we can sing it as the aspiration of our heart. And although we may never realize total commitment, we can seek to maximize the extent to which our lives are turned over to the Lord.

22
A Living Sacrifice

Arguably the outstanding passage in the New Testament exhorting believers to a life of full commitment is Romans 12:1-2:

> I beseech you therefore, brethren, by the mercies of God, that you present your bodies a living sacrifice, holy, acceptable to God, which is your reasonable service. And do not be conformed to this world, but be transformed by the renewing of your mind, that you may prove what is that good and acceptable and perfect will of God.

When my brother and I were boys, and H. A. Ironside was visiting in our home, he taught us a chorus based on the first verse:

> *Romans twelve and one is a verse I will not shun,*
> *But yield to Him alone who is there upon the throne;*
> *If He's not Lord of all, then He's not Lord at all.*
> *Romans twelve and one.*

Many times in the years that followed, I have realized how far short I fell from the ideal expressed in the phrase "Lord of all," but I have sought to make it the aspiration of my heart.

Every word in that golden text is charged with meaning. Put them all together and we have the key to the abundant life which the Lord Jesus promised.

The Voice of God

In Romans 12:1, who is saying, "I beseech you"? To whom does the *I* refer? Well, it obviously refers to Paul, since he is the author

129

of the letter. He is the one who said, "For to me, to live is Christ" (Phil. 1:21). And "The love of Christ compels us, because we judge thus: that if One died for all, then all died, and He died for all, that those who live should no longer live for themselves, but for Him who died for them and rose again" (2 Cor. 5:14-15). Paul said he forgot the things that were behind, and reached forward to the things that were ahead. He pressed toward the mark for the prize of the upward call of God in Christ Jesus (Phil. 3:13-14).

But we must remember that Paul was writing this by divine revelation. The words were not only his words, but the words of the Lord. The same Lord said, "I must work the works of Him who sent me while it is day" (John 9:4). And, "My food is to do the will of Him who sent Me, and to finish His work" (John 4:34).

Notice next the word *beseech.* God is beseeching you and me. The word has a stronger force than *ask.* It expresses urgency and importunity. There are overtones of imploring and pleading. It describes a centurion who pled with Jesus to heal his servant (Mt. 8:5-6). Sick people besought Jesus to heal them (Mt. 14:35, 36). A leper besought the Lord to make him clean (Mark 1:40). It's what Jairus did when he begged the Lord to heal his dying daughter (Mark 5:22, 23). It's what Paul did when he besought sinners to be reconciled to God (2 Cor. 5:20). So if you listen carefully, you will hear the compassionate heartbeat of God, urging His people to actions that will ensure the best possible life. He wants to save us from a wasted life, from a life devoted to trivia.

In the obituary column of a local newspaper, the following sentences described the central point in the lives of some who had passed away:

• "He had a way with pumpkins and was born with a long family tradition of celebrating Halloween to the hilt, honing his pumpkin-carving skills at a young age."
• "She enjoyed TV, especially Jeopardy."
• "He enjoyed Bingo, coffee and toast in the morning at local restaurants, small children, his garden, and fruit, and cool water."

Those are all harmless activities, but is that all there is to life?

After the resurrection, Peter had the marvelous privilege of preaching the message that the world so sorely needed. But what did he say? "I am going fishing" (John 21:3).

God wants to save us from spending our lives in the study of the sleeping habits of Puerto Rican lizards or the primary function of the picnic in modern society, as some have done.

"I beseech you therefore, brethren." The word *therefore* is a connective. It alerts us to recognize that what God is about to say is closely related to what He has said previously."You...brethren" makes it obvious that the urgent appeal is addressed to all Christians. *Brethren* here is a generic word, embracing male and female, young and old, recent converts and mature saints. No one who has experienced Christ's redemption is excluded.

The Mercies of God

"By the mercies of God." This phrase tells us what the appeal is based on. Paul had just finished reviewing many of the marvelous mercies which come through faith in the Lord Jesus. Let us list some of them:

• We were foreknown by God (Rom. 8:29). That is how it all began. In compassionate mercy He set in motion His plans for eternal salvation. But each of us has to ask, "Why me?"

• He predestined believers to be eventually conformed to the image of His Son (Rom. 8:29). Such grace is unthinkable but wonderfully true.

• God called us (Rom. 8:30). He providentially arranged that we should hear the gospel and have the opportunity to respond by faith. Again we marvel, in the words of Isaac Watts:

> *Why was I made to hear Thy voice*
> *And enter while there's room,*
> *While thousands make a wretched choice*
> *And rather starve than come?*

131

• He justified us (Rom. 8:30). That means He cleared us of every charge. This is more than pardon or forgiveness. It is as if there had never been any charge against us. The record is clear. We stand before Him in His righteousness because we are in Christ.

• We have been reconciled to God (Rom. 5:10-11). The cause of the conflict was our sin. The Lord Jesus removed the cause by putting away those sins by the sacrifice of Himself. Who but God could have ever conceived this plan of salvation?

• We have access by faith into a wonderful position of favor with God (Rom. 5:2). He is now our Father and we are His children. He accepts us in the Beloved; therefore we are as near and dear to God as His beloved Son.

• We are indwelt by the Holy Spirit of God (Rom. 8:9). Our bodies are actually the temples of the Third Person of the Trinity. Just think of that!

• We have assurance of our salvation by the Holy Spirit's witness to us through the Word of God (Rom. 8:16). We are not left to the vagaries of human emotions. We can know we are saved, whether we feel it or not.

• We are eternally secure (Rom. 5:6-10). Since Christ went to such enormous cost to save us from the penalty of sin, He will never let us go. He lives at the right hand of God to guarantee our preservation (Rom. 8:34). That is fail-safe security.

• Now we have peace with God through our Lord Jesus Christ (Rom. 5:1). This peace is completely independent of circumstances. It is an other-worldly serenity that comes from knowing that the sin question has been settled and the Lord is in control.

• As if that isn't enough, we are heirs of God and joint heirs with Jesus Christ (Rom. 8:17). All that the Father has is ours. Such wealth cannot be counted; it is more than we can imagine.

• We are sanctified, that is, set apart to God from the world and from sin. By the Holy Spirit we can have deliverance from the power of indwelling sin—a marvelous deliverance (8:1-4).

• We are not under the law but under grace (Rom. 6:14). The law ordered us to obey but didn't give us the power to do it, and condemned us if we failed. Grace teaches us what to do, gives us the power to do it, and rewards us when we do. You can't beat that.

• We are enabled to rejoice in tribulations because we know that the Lord uses them to develop character in our lives (Rom. 5:3, 4). He works all things together for good to those who love Him. The good is that we should become more Christlike.

• We have a wonderful hope. Paul calls it the hope of the glory of God (Rom. 5:2). It means being in heaven with the Lord in all His beauty and magnificence. It also means that we will have glorified bodies, just like the body which Jesus has in resurrection.

• We have the assurance that nothing can ever separate us from the love of God which is in Christ Jesus our Lord (Rom. 8:35-39). We are as sure of heaven as if we were already there.

All these promises are a sample of what is included in the mercies of God, although they don't exhaust that phrase. Now, then, back to verse 1 of Romans chapter 12.

The Only Reasonable Response

These mercies of God should constrain us to present our bodies in an act of thanksgiving and worship. The logic of it is expressed in the poem:

> *After all He's done for me,*
> *After all He's done for me,*
> *How can I do less than give Him my best*
> *And live for Him completely*
> *After all He's done for me?*
>
> —Betty Daasvand

Why does Paul say "your bodies"? Why not our spirits or souls? Because God knows that if we give Him our bodies we are giving Him ourselves. Our bodies are the medium by which we express ourselves. So the body here stands for the complete person. We should also note that the apostle is comparing and contrasting our sacrifice with the animal sacrifices of the Old Testament; it was the bodies that were placed on the altar.[1]

The believer's body is to be presented as "a living sacrifice." This is in contrast to the dead sacrifices which Israel offered. It also includes the thought that whereas an animal sacrifice was offered only once, our sacrifice is to be a continual offering.

When we present our body, that includes all our members: hands, eyes, ears, mouth, brain. In a day of sexual promiscuity, it is good to remind ourselves that it includes the procreative members also. It includes our talents, such as music, poetry, art, eloquence. We give Him our knowledge in the sciences, history, philosophy, logic. When we do, we can look back and see how He guided us in our education, often taking courses when we did not know why, but He knew, and He was preparing us for His service.

The sacrifice of ourselves must be holy and acceptable to God. It is not enough that we are "positionally sanctified," that God sees us as holy because we are in Christ. We must be practically sanctified, that is, our lives must be clean. This answers to the Old Testament requirement that animals offered to God must be without spot or blemish. When believers confess and forsake all known sin, then their offering of their lives is pleasing to God.

The last clause of Romans 12:1 may be translated in two ways: "which is your reasonable service" (NKJV) or "which is your spiritual act of worship" (NIV). Both make good sense. To present our bodies to Christ is the most sane, sensible, reasonable thing we can do in the light of what He has done for us. But it is also an act of worship. As holy priests, we present to God our praise (Heb. 13:15), our possessions (Heb. 13:16), our service (Rom. 15:16), and now our person. Offering our bodies is the greatest act of worship of which we are capable.

Living sacrifices must not be conformed to the world. J. B. Phillips' oft-quoted paraphrase says it well: "Don't let the world around you squeeze you into its own mold." The world in this sense is human society that not only seeks to be independent of God but is actively hostile to Him. It has its own belief system, value system, lifestyles, motives, and ambitions, and it wants everyone to conform to them. Those who would be acceptable to God must be non-conformists.

The world says, "This above all else, to your own dear self be true." Or, "I am the master of my fate: I am the captain of my soul." It says, "If it feels good, do it." Or "You only live once." "The one who dies with the most toys wins." "There is no absolute truth; everything is relative." "We have all evolved from primordial slime." "Immorality and other so-called deviant behavior are not sin but sickness." "Law-breakers are not criminals; they are victims."

We Christians must reject such thinking and be transformed by the renewing of our minds. In other words, we must learn to think the way God thinks, as revealed in the Scriptures. This will result in a transformation of our interests, speech, dress, and music. We will have a new mind-set toward other people, wealth, success, politics, and sexuality. Our thought life will be revolutionized.

The Key to Guidance

Now in verse 2 of Romans 12, we discover the sure way to know the guidance of God. It is by full surrender of ourselves to the Lord for whatever He may choose. We not only discern His will, but we discover by experience that it is not at all what we had feared: disagreeable, difficult, and dangerous. Instead, we find it to be good, acceptable, and perfect. It is beneficial, pleasant, and ideal. Since it is God's will, it can be nothing less than perfect.

Now let us go back to the beginning of Romans 12 and review the flow of thought: The mercies of God require that believers should present themselves as a continual offering to Him. The offering, of course, must be holy; otherwise it would not be pleasing to Him. Total commitment is the most reasonable response that Chris-

135

tians can make to the Saviour's sacrifice. It is also the most appropriate act of worship. For the offering of believers to be acceptable, they must avoid being molded by the world. Rather they must adopt a godly mind-set and lifestyle.

It stands to reason that if we put the Lord in control, our life will be the best that divine wisdom can plan. We will have a life that is good for us, pleasing to God, and ideal in every respect.

Here are the words of a living sacrifice:

> *In full and glad surrender, I give myself to Thee,*
> *Thine utterly and only and evermore to be!*
> *O Son of God who lovest me, I will be Thine alone,*
> *And all I am and all I have shall henceforth be Thine own.*
> —F. R. Havergal

Lord, I surrender all. All this Thou hast done for me. It is a reasonable service, that I no longer have plans of my own.

ENDNOTE

1 There might also be a striking contrast between our bodies and minds given for the Lord's use (v. 2) with the bodies and minds given over to sin in Romans 1 (*ed.*).

23
Reasons for Full Surrender

Those who are true Christians know what it is to turn over their lives to the Lord Jesus for salvation. They have been convicted of their sin and their unfitness for God's presence. They have believed that the Saviour died to pay the penalty of all their sins. They have turned themselves over to Him to save them for all eternity. It is all so reasonable. Salvation is a free gift. It is theirs for the taking. They have everything to gain and nothing to lose. They would be fools not to accept Christ and be sure of heaven.

But it is possible to accept Christ for salvation and yet not surrender ourselves to Him for service. We can trust Him to take us to heaven but somehow we can't trust Him to manage our lives here on earth. We have our own plans and ambitions, and we don't want anyone or anything to interfere with them. We gladly acknowledge Christ as Saviour of our souls, but hold back from crowning Him King of our lives.

Because of the heavy emphasis placed on evangelism in the Church today, it is possible that when a person is saved, he feels that there's nothing more to do. We must disabuse ourselves of the idea that conversion is the final goal. As far as fitness for heaven is concerned, our new birth is all that is necessary. But it is not the ultimate in the Christian life. We must move on to a day-by-day walk in full surrender to the Lordship of Christ.

We need to face some facts and consider their logic. Every indicative in God's plan of redemption carries with it an imperative. Doctrines lead to duty. We must marvel at the truths that flow from

Calvary and decide what we are going to do about them.

Our Creator Died to Save Us

First of all, nothing can overshadow the incredible reality that the One who died on the cross was no less than God incarnate. It was the Creator dying for His creatures, the Judge dying for the criminals, the Holy One dying for sinners. When God's Son died, the Lover died for His enemies, the Guiltless for the guilty, the Rich One for the poor. Once we really come to grips with this astonishing fact, we can never be the same again. We will be overwhelmed. Anything short of our full dedication is a denial of the enormous meaning of Calvary. Let it burn into our souls that Someone paid the ultimate price for us, and that Someone is the One who designed the universe and everything in it. Then our hearts will respond:

> *Thus might I hide my blushing face*
> *While His dear cross appears;*
> *Dissolve my heart in thankfulness*
> *And melt my eyes to tears.*
>
> *But drops of grief can ne'er repay*
> *The debt of love I owe;*
> *Dear Lord, I give myself away—*
> *'Tis all that I can do.*
>
> —Isaac Watts

The Mercies of God

A second consideration is this: the mercies of God demand that we yield our entire being to Him. When we speak of the mercies of God, we mean the marvelous privileges, positions, and favors He has conferred on believers. We mean all the benefits that were purchased for us at Calvary. We have listed some of them in a previous chapter.

No mere mortal would ever have the audacity to conceive such a list of kindnesses to people so unworthy. It is a catalog of spiritual largesse that we did not seek and could not purchase. But it came to us without cost in the gift of eternal life. The more we meditate on the mercies of God, the more baffled we are that He would endow us so handsomely.

The French have a saying, *noblesse oblige,* that is, nobility obligates. People who are of high birth or rank are obligated to respond appropriately. Christians are certainly of high birth (born into God's family) and of high rank (heirs of God and joint heirs with Jesus Christ). The proper response is to yield control of their lives to the Father of mercies. They should present their bodies to Him as a living sacrifice.

Gratitude Demands It

A third reason for our full commitment is gratitude. If thankfulness is appropriate for someone who saves us from drowning or from a burning building, what is the proper response to the One who has given His body to save us from hell? There is only one answer: As we hear Him say, "This is my body given for you," what could be more proper than for us to say, "Thank You, Lord Jesus. This is my body, my heart, my life, my all, given for You"?

When missionary J. Alexander Clark saw an African being attacked by a lion, he grabbed his gun, killed the lion, took the man to the hospital, and cared for him until he was well enough to go back to his tribe. Two or three months later, Clark was sitting on his veranda when he heard a terrific commotion: hens clucking, ducks quacking, sheep bleating, and the gabble of men, women, and children. Here was a tall African leading a parade of animals, poultry, and people. It was the man whom Clark had saved from the jaws of the lion. Falling at the missionary's feet, the man said, "Sir, according to the laws of my tribe, the man who has been rescued from a wild beast no longer belongs to himself. He belongs to his saviour. All that I have is yours: my chickens, ducks, goats, sheep, cows— they are all yours. My servants are your servants. My children (he had quite a few) are your children, and my wives (he had several) are your wives. Everything I have is yours."[1]

It was just a matter of simple gratitude, that's all.

139

The Love of Christ Compels It

There is a fourth reason also why full surrender is the most reasonable, rational, logical thing we can do. Paul tells how the love of Christ compels us.

> For the love of Christ constraineth us, because we thus judge, that if one died for all, then were all dead: and that He died for all, that they which live should not henceforth live unto themselves but unto Him which died for them, and rose again (2 Cor.5:14-15, KJV).

Let me break it down into a series of simple statements:

- We were all dead in trespasses and sins.
- The Lord Jesus died for us so that we might live.
- But He didn't die for us so that we would live self-centered and self-directed lives.
- Instead He wants us to live for Him who died for us.

It makes good sense—doesn't it? Let's take a break just to think about that love for a while.

It is eternal, the only love that is unoriginated. It is age-abiding and unending. Our minds strain to comprehend a love that is ceaseless and unremitting.

It is immeasurable. Its height, depth, length, and breadth are infinite. Nowhere do we find such extravagance. Poets have compared it to creation's greatest expanses, but the words always seem to bend under the weight of the idea.

Christ's love to us is causeless and unprovoked. He could see nothing lovable or meritorious in us to draw out His affections, yet He loved us just the same. He did it because that's the way He is.

Our love for others is often based on ignorance. We love people because we don't really know what they are like. We judge them by their appearance, but the more we get to know them, the more we are aware of their faults and failures, and then the less likable they appear. But the Lord Jesus loved us even when He knew all that we would ever be or do. His omniscience did not cancel His love.

But there are so many people in the world—over five billion. Can the Sovereign God love each one personally?

> *Among so many, can He care?*
> *Can special love be everywhere?*

With Him there are no nobodies. No one is insignificant. His affection flows out to every individual on the planet.

Such love is incomparable. Most people know the love of a devoted mother. Or the faithful love of a wife or husband. David knew the love of Jonathan. Jesus knew the love of John. But no one has ever experienced anything human that can compare with the divine love. As a hymn reminds us, "No one ever cared for me like Jesus."

In Romans 8, Paul ransacks the universe for anything that might separate a believer from the love of Jesus, but he comes up empty. Neither death, life, angels, principalities, powers, things present nor things to come, height, depth, nor any created thing can divorce us from God's love.

It is awesome to realize that the omnipotent One cannot love you or me more than He does at this moment. His love is absolutely unrestrained and unreserved. In a world of constant flux, it is assuring to find something that is unchanging: namely, the love of Christ. Our love moves in cycles. It is an emotional roller coaster. Not so with our Lord. His love never tires or varies. It is constant.

His love is a pure love, free from selfishness, unrighteous compromise, or unworthy motive. It is untainted and without a touch of defilement. And like His grace, the love of Jesus is free. For this we can be everlastingly thankful because we are paupers, beggars, and bankrupt sinners. Even if we owned all the wealth in the world, we still could never put even a down payment on so priceless a love.

Here is a love that is impartial. It causes the sun to shine on the just and the unjust. It orders the rain to fall without discrimination.

His love manifests itself in giving. "Christ also loved the church and gave..." Since it is more blessed to give than to receive, the Lord always has the prerogative of being the more blessed.

One of the most amazing things about it is that it is sacrificial. It led Him to Calvary, its greatest demonstration. At the cross we see a love that is stronger than death, that not even the billows of God's wrath could drown.

This unique love surpasses our powers of description. It is sublime, matchless, the Everest of affections. Our present dictionary is not adequate to picture it. There are not enough adjectives—simple, comparative, and superlative. We can go only so far; then we have to say what the Queen of Sheba said about the glory of Solomon: "The half has not been told." The subject surpasses human language.

We may search the universe for a better dictionary, an enlarged vocabulary, but it would be in vain. Not until we reach heaven and gaze on Incarnate Love will we see with clearer vision, understand with keener intellect, the love of the Lord Jesus Christ for us. Even then, the subject will not be exhausted.

This is the kind of love that constrains us to live for Him who died for us.

> *Love so amazing, so divine*
> *Demands my heart, my life, my all.*

Lady Powerscourt, an English Christian of nobility put it rather bluntly: "It seems an insult to that love which gave ALL for us, to say we love, and yet stop to calculate about giving all to Him. Our all is but two mites. His all is heaven, earth, eternity, Himself. Better not to love at all. Better to be cold than lukewarm."

> *Dear Cross, I hear thy pleading voice;*
> *To spurn I cannot move.*
> *My heart is conquered, take my all,*
> *For less insults thy love.*
> —J. Sidlow Baxter

We Are Not Our Own

Fifth, simple honesty demands that we surrender our lives to

Him. Our Lord Jesus purchased us at Calvary. He paid an enormous price—His own blood. Now if He bought us, we no longer belong to ourselves. We belong to Him. It is one of the delightful paradoxes of Christianity that although all things are ours (1 Cor. 3:21), yet we are not our own. It follows that if we take our lives and do what we want with them, we are taking something that doesn't belong to us. There is a word for that. It is called theft. Full surrender saves us from being thieves. When C. T. Studd saw this, he wrote:

> I had known about Jesus dying for me, but I had never understood that if He died for me, then I didn't belong to myself. Redemption means buying back, so that if I belong to Him, either I had to be a thief and keep what wasn't mine, or else I had to give up everything to God. When I came to see that Jesus had died for me, it didn't seem hard to give up all for Him.

The logic is incontrovertible, isn't it? But what are we going to do about it?

Oswald Sanders told of a church organist in Germany who was very possessive of his organ. He made it a point not to allow others to use it. One sunny afternoon he was practicing a piece by Felix Mendelssohn, and not playing it well. Unknown to him, however, a stranger stole into the church and sat in the shadows of the back pew. He couldn't help but notice the difficulty the organist was having. When the organist finally gave up and gathered his music to leave, the visitor went forward and courteously asked permission to play. The answer was blunt. The organist never allowed anyone else to play. Again the visitor requested the privilege and again he was rebuffed.

But his persistence paid off. The third time he asked, he was allowed to do so, even if grudgingly.

He sat down, arranged the stops, and played the same piece. Immediately the church was filled with the most beautiful harmony. At the close, the amazed organist asked, "Who are you?"

The visitor modestly bowed his head, then said, "I am Felix Mendelssohn."

"What!" said the organist, completely nonplussed. "Did I refuse *you* permission to play on my organ?"

Our lives are God's organ, not our own. Should we refuse Him permission to play on it?

Jesus Is Lord

Let us move on to a sixth reason for presenting all that we are and have to the Lord and allowing Him to run our lives. We call Him Lord. "To this end Christ died...and lived again, that He might be Lord" (Rom. 14:9). If He is Lord, He has a right to all. If Christ is not Lord in a person's life, then that person does what is right in his own eyes. It is not without significance that whereas the word *Saviour* is found 24 times in the New Testament, the word *Lord* is found almost 670 times! Although we commonly say "Saviour and Lord," the Bible never does. It always says "Lord and Saviour." It reverses the order. Peter reminds us that we should sanctify Christ as Lord in our hearts (1 Pet. 3:15), that is, set Him apart as Master.

When Joshua was preparing for the assault on Jericho, a Man appeared to Him, sword in hand. Before Joshua realized who the Man was, he asked, "Are you for us or against us?" The Man replied, in effect, "I didn't come to be for you or against you. I came to take over." "...as Commander of the army of the Lord I have now come" (Josh. 5:14). Then Joshua realized that he was talking to the Lord. It was Jesus in a pre-incarnate appearance. Joshua fell on His face, worshiped Him, addressed Him as Lord, and submitted to His leadership.

Here is a great lesson for us. The Saviour does not come into our lives simply to be on our side, and He certainly doesn't come to be our adversary. He wants to be Lord, to take over, to be Commander-in-chief. How can I call Him Lord, yet refuse Him when He calls me to full surrender? We must do what He says or stop calling Him Lord.

He Knows Better than We Do

Seventh, there is something else to think about. We act as if we know what is the best plan for our lives. We choose our occupation, set our goals, and proceed with our own ambitions. We overlook the fact that Christ might have *something infinitely better.* He can work out a better life than we could ever dream of. God is wonderfully creative. He has a fantastic imagination. He knows options of which we are unaware. He wants only the best for His people, so His blueprint is filtered through His infinite love and wisdom. The contrast between His outlook and ours is stark:

> *I counted dollars while God counted crosses!*
> *I counted gains while He counted losses!*
> *I counted my worth by the things gained in store,*
> *He sized me up by the scars that I wore.*
> *I counted honors and sought for degrees!*
> *He wept as He counted the hours on my knees.*
> *I never knew till one day by the grave*
> *How vain are the things we spend life to save.*
> —Author unknown

Unless we surrender our lives to Him, we are showing Him that strange disrespect of preferring our own intelligence to His, of saying that we know better than He does.

What Refusal Really Is

R. A. Laidlaw, author of the widely-used booklet *The Reason Why,* adds an eighth consideration: "There is a lack of sincerity in committing the eternal soul to God for salvation and then holding back the mortal life. We dare to trust Him to save us from hell and to take us to heaven, but we hesitate to let Him control our lives here and now."

In addressing young people, a Keswick speaker said this: "People will call you nutty if you are fully committed to Christ. I say, 'Be as nutty as you can be for Jesus Christ.' I'll tell you who the nutty ones are. They are those who stand in the shadow of Calvary, who look into the face of the dying Redeemer as He purchases them with His blood, and then go out to do the things they want to do, to

145

live the way they want to live."
Here then is the logic of full surrender:

> *What shall I give Thee, Master?*
> *Thou who has died for me.*
> *Shall I give less than all I possess,*
> *Or shall I give all to Thee?*
> *Jesus, my Lord and Saviour,*
> *Thou hast given all for me.*
> *Not just a part, or half of my heart,*
> *I will give all to Thee.*

—Homer W. Grimes

ENDNOTE

1 Chua Wee Hian, *I Saw the Lord, The Cross and the Crown,* Carlisle, England: OM Publishing, 1992, pp. 134-135.

24
A Squirming Sacrifice

Isn't it strange that when God calls a person, the normal instinct is to resist?

When the Lord commissioned Moses to demand deliverance for His people, the patriarch protested, "Who am I that I should go to Pharaoh, and that I should bring the children of Israel out of Egypt?" (Ex. 3:11). Later, he added another excuse: "O my Lord, I am not eloquent, neither before or since Thou hast spoken to Thy servant; but I am slow of speech and slow of tongue" (Ex. 4:10). Jeremiah also argued against the Lord's choice of him: "Ah, Lord God! Behold, I cannot speak, for I am a youth" (Jer. 1:6).

In a New Testament parable, a nobleman entrusted ten servants with money to invest. But they hated him, saying, "We will not have this man to reign over us" (Luke 19:14). Saul of Tarsus stubbornly resisted the convicting power of the Holy Spirit, as is evident from the Saviour's words, "It is hard for you to kick against the goads" (Acts 9:5).

C. S. Lewis said that the Lord brought him in kicking and screaming, "the most reluctant convert in all England." Many of us can understand exactly what he meant, because that too was our experience.

Rebellion

For years we had gone astray, like sheep that wanted nothing more than to have their own way. Stomping our foot, we shouted defiantly, "We will not have this Man to rule over us." We were determined that no one would direct our lives or interfere with our plans and ambitions.

We wanted pleasure, and were convinced that God didn't want us to have it. He was the cosmic spoilsport. We wanted the approval of our companions; we cared nothing for divine approval. We wanted self to be on the throne, and looked upon the Lord as the meddling usurper.

Then gradually our peace was shattered. Looking back, it must have been that someone was praying for us. Without any desire on our part, we began to meet people who wouldn't mind their own business. They insisted on confronting us with God and Jesus, sin and salvation, heaven and hell. It didn't matter whether we were at work or in a shopping mall. Christians would pass tracts to us. We would see "Jesus Saves" painted on a rock. Often when we turned on the radio or TV, we would hear some mention of God or of heaven or of hell. It seemed that religion was everywhere, as common as a phone booth or a Coca Cola sign.

War Breaks Out

Open warfare erupted. We asked Him to leave us alone. Like Saul of Tarsus, we were kicking against the goads, and it was hard. In one sense, we were at war with the Omnipotent One, but it also seemed that we were running away from Him. In our insanity, we were trying to flee from the One who is omnipresent. Francis Thompson pictured our flight in *The Hound of Heaven:*

> *I fled Him, down the nights and down the days;*
> *I fled Him, down the arches of the years;*
> *I fled Him, down the labyrinthine ways*
> *Of my own mind; and in the mist of tears*
> *I hid from Him, and under running laughter.*
> *Up vistaed hopes, I sped;*
> *And shot, precipitated,*
> *Adown titanic glooms of chasmed fears,*
> *From those strong feet that followed, followed after.*

But with unhurrying chase,
And unperturbed pace,
Deliberate speed, majestic instancy,
They beat—and a Voice beat
More instant than the Feet—
"All things betray thee, who betrayest Me."

It was irrational. We were fighting against our own best interests. We thought the Saviour wanted to rob us of pleasure when He wanted us to enjoy true pleasure. We thought His will was bad, undesirable, and horrible. Actually it was the best in every way. He wanted to save us from the sins that were dragging us down to hell. He wanted to give us eternal life as a free gift. He did not come to steal, kill, or destroy, but to give us life more abundantly.

It reminds me of a radio preacher who was getting ready to retire for the night when the phone rang. It was a grateful and enthusiastic listener to his program. She had time between two trains and wanted to visit him and his wife. He brought up all kinds of difficulties. It was a long way from the station. She said she would take a bus. But, he warned, the buses stopped operating in half an hour. Not to worry: she would take a taxi.

Finally running out of excuses, he told her to come. The taxi arrived. She came to the door and stayed for only a short time. As she left, she pressed a wad of money into his hand. All she wanted was to help him buy time for the radio program.

Later he confessed, "I'm so glad I let her in."

So it was with us. Christ came knocking at our door in sunshine and rain. We controlled the door knob and kept Him locked out. We didn't treat our friends and neighbors that way. All He wanted was to give us life eternal.

Futile Search

We raced around trying to find pleasure. We were drinking at broken cisterns. But Christ offered us water which, if we drank of it, we would never thirst again. We wanted our sins more than we wanted Christ.

There were moments when we actually weakened, when we thought that maybe we should accept the Saviour. After all, the preacher said we had everything to gain and nothing to lose. But what would our friends think? We were ashamed. Ashamed of Jesus. The thought of confessing Him before others sent chills down our spine. No, we could never tell people we had been saved, we had been born again. We could hear their sneering laughs and belittling remarks. Already we could see their snide glances.

Conviction

By this time, conviction of sin was deepening. Day and night God's hand was heavy upon us. Like David, our "vitality was turned into the drought of summer" (Ps. 32:4). If we tried to plead our basic goodness, the Spirit of God would remind us of our thought-life. It became obvious that no one with a polluted mind like ours could ever enter the kingdom of God. When we should be sleeping, we were wide awake, conscious of a load of sin on our shoulders and fearful of the just punishment that awaited us. Hell was no longer only a swear word that we used carelessly; it was a terrible reality.

With hypocritical skill, we tried to hide from our friends the emotions that were surging through our souls. What good actors we were. Yet we were consumed by fear and confusion, a tangled mass of contradictions. To put it bluntly, our life was falling apart. Like C. S. Lewis, we felt "the steady, unrelenting approach of Him whom (we) so earnestly desired not to meet."

Salvation

Then at last came the day we had dreaded. Stripped of strength and pride, we dejectedly bleated out our unconditional surrender:

> *Nay, but I yield, I yield;*
> *I can hold out no more,*
> *I sink by dying love compelled*
> *And own Thee conqueror.*

150

Perhaps it happened when the Christians were singing Charlotte Elliott's hymn:

> *Just as I am, without one plea,*
> *But that Thy blood was shed for me,*
> *And that Thou bidd'st me come to Thee,*
> *O Lamb of God, I come! I come!*
>
> *Just as I am, and waiting not*
> *To rid my soul of one dark blot,*
> *To Thee whose blood can cleanse each spot,*
> *O Lamb of God, I come! I come!*
>
> *Just as I am, tho' tossed about*
> *With many a conflict, many a doubt,*
> *Fightings within and fears without*
> *O Lamb of God, I come! I come!*
>
> *Just as I am, poor, wretched, blind;*
> *Sight, riches, healing of the mind,*
> *Yes, all I need in Thee to find,*
> *O Lamb of God, I come! I come!*
>
> *Just as I am, Thou wilt receive,*
> *Wilt welcome, pardon, cleanse, relieve,*
> *Because Thy promise I believe;*
> *O Lamb of God, I come! I come!*
>
> *Just as I am, Thy love unknown*
> *Hath broken ev'ry barrier down;*
> *Now to be Thine, yea Thine alone,*
> *O Lamb of God, I come! I come!*

The chase was over. The Hound of Heaven had caught up with us. We lay panting at the foot of the cross, weak and helpless. It no longer mattered what our friends thought of us, only what He thought of us. In that moment it dawned on us that our supposed Enemy and Pursuer was in reality our Best Friend. Our fears had been groundless. In running from the Lord, we had actually been afraid of a blessing.

The war was over. We now had peace with God through the Lord Jesus Christ. We were now on the Victor's side. And those irritating Christians who used to buttonhole us—all of a sudden they were our brothers and sisters to whom we felt deep gratitude.

Lewis asks, "Who can duly adore that Love which will open the high gates to a prodigal who is brought in kicking, struggling, resentful, and darting his eyes in every direction for a chance to escape?"

A New Battle

But another battle had begun. True, we had trusted the Lord for the eternal salvation of our souls. But now we faced another question. Would we surrender our lives to Him for service? Could we trust Him to manage our lives here on earth?

Once more our stubborn wills shifted into high gear. We knew what we should do, but we weren't prepared to do it. We knew that divine logic pointed to full surrender, but that might interfere with what we had mapped out for our future: an idyllic marriage with good-looking children; a profession or occupation that would yield a good income and a reputation for success in the community; a better-than-average house in the suburbs; comfort, security, pleasure— and, O yes—some time for service for the Lord.

To all outward appearances, the world was our oyster. Everything was going our way. Our relatives and friends were clucking over our success. What they didn't know was that there was a deep disquiet in our hearts. We felt as if we were chasing shadows. Under the surface we were struggling with the issue of full surrender.

We were afraid. Afraid of what His will for us might be. Certainly it couldn't be as glamorous as the life we had carved out for ourselves. We duelled with God and listened to our hesitations too long. It never dawned on us that the Lord had options for us that were better than we could imagine. Options in which we could find fulfillment. Options that would make us deliriously happy.

Surrender

Finally we realized our foolishness. The Holy Spirit removed the blinders from our eyes. We saw that the God of infinite love wants nothing but the best for His people. We tumbled to the fact that His will is best. And so we did something we had never done before. For the first time, we bowed our knees and turned ourselves over to Him as a living sacrifice. We said, in effect: "Anywhere, Lord. Any time. Anything." It was so logical. It made such good sense. How could we do less than give Him our best and live for Him completely, after all He's done for us?

We had already turned our lives over to Him for salvation. Now we turned them over to Him for service. We said:

> *Jesus, Lord and Master, love divine has conquered,*
> *I will henceforth answer Yes, to all Thy will.*
> *Free from Satan's bondage, I am Thine forever;*
> *Henceforth all Thy purposes in me fulfill.*
> —E. H. Swinstead

But as time went on, we learned a painful lesson. Our living sacrifice had a wretched tendency to crawl off the altar. It was a squirming sacrifice at best.

We realized that the crisis of surrender was not enough. The once-for-all commitment had to be followed by continual commitment. Each morning we had to come to the Lord and renew our consecration. Each morning we had to exchange our will for His. And so we began on a daily basis to kneel at our bed and say, "Lord Jesus, I rededicate myself to You for the next twenty-four hours."

Then as His will unfolded, we found the real reason for our existence. We found a new peace and poise in our lives. We were humbly conscious that God was working in and through us, and that when our life touched other lives, something happened for God.

Having turned our lives over to the Lord, we went through the day believing that He was guiding us, controlling us, and using us.

Looking back, we see how accurately Theodore Monod captured the story of our squirming sacrifice in these lines:

Oh, the bitter shame and sorrow
That a time could ever be,
When I let the Saviour's pity
Plead in vain, and proudly answered,
All of self, and none of Thee.

Yet He found me; I beheld Him
Bleeding on the cursed tree;
Heard Him pray, Forgive them, Father,
And my wistful heart said faintly,
Some of self, and some of Thee.

Day by day His tender mercy,
Healing, helping, full and free,
Sweet and strong and ah! so patient,
Brought me lower while I whispered,
Less of self, and more of Thee.

Higher than the highest heavens,
Deeper than the deepest sea,
Lord, Thy love at last hath conquered:
Grant me now my soul's petition,
None of self, and all of Thee.

25
Trivial Pursuits

When Christ is at the controls, He saves us from spending our lives on trivia. He guarantees that they will be of eternal consequence. We may not realize it at the time, but it's true nonetheless.

One of the pains of living is to see people who were made in the image of God wasting their time on trivial pursuits. It is especially sad to see Christians prostituting their strength and talents on something that doesn't matter.

How to Waste a Life

With a world perishing, who in his right mind would want to give the best of his life analyzing the microbic content of cotton T-shirts? Or the browning reaction of potato chips? Or mineral deficiencies in the tomato and cocklebur? It's one thing to work with potato chips and cockleburs in order to provide for one's family. But it is something else to make doing that the central thing in life.

Corrie Ten Boom wrote: "When a house is on fire and you know that there are people in it, it is a sin to straighten the pictures in that house. When the world about you is in great danger, works that in themselves are not sinful can be quite wrong."

Vance Havner said that many people like that "drown in mud puddles of insignificant issues and have no time for great concerns. And when they pass off the scene, it's as if they had never lived at all." Life has been not so much the transit of a man but what Jowett called "the passage of an amoeba."

How apropos are the words of Cornelius Plantinga, Jr:

Making a career of Nothing—wandering through malls, killing time, making small talk, watching television programs until we know their characters better than our own children...shapes life into a yawn at the God and Saviour of the world. The person who will not bestir herself, the person who hands herself over to Nothing, in effect says to God: You have made nothing of interest and redeemed no one of consequence, including me.[1]

Is That All There Is?

Is there nothing better in life than to score goals in a football game? Must we climb to the top of a worldly ambition and find that there's nothing there?

Even the apostle Peter seemed to forget his priorities at an important point in his life. The Lord Jesus had risen from the dead. The world desperately needed to hear the message of salvation through faith in Him. Peter's main concern was fishing in the Sea of Galilee. Times haven't changed. We hear the message that will bring forgiveness of sins and eternity in heaven, and we say, "I'm going golfing."

I often think how James Dobson learned a valuable lesson through the game of *Monopoly*:

Recently my family played Monopoly, which was the first time I've played it in fifteen years. Before long, a bit of the old excitement and enthusiasm came back, especially as I began to win. Everything went my way, and I became master of the board. I owned Boardwalk and Park Place, and I had houses and hotels all over the place. My family was squirming, and I was stuffing $500 bills into my pockets and under the board and seat. Suddenly the game was over. I had won. Shirley and the kids went to bed, and I began putting everything back into the box. Then I was struck by an empty feeling. All of the excitement I had experienced earlier was unfounded. I didn't own any more than those whom I had defeated. It all had to go back into the box!

The Lord showed me that there was a lesson to be learned beyond the game of Monopoly. I recognized that I was also witnessing the game of life. We struggle and accumulate and buy and own and possess and refinance, and suddenly we come to the end of life and have to put it all back into the box! We can't take a cent with us! There are no trailers that accompany us through the Valley of the Shadow.[2]

It's time we put away the fun and games. The vision of Christ on the cross should deliver us from trivia and set our sights on goals of eternal significance.

In his book *The Hidden Life,* Adolf Saphir had a special appeal to young people:

Let not your biography be summed up: "He turned to God in his youth, he then became lukewarm, being engrossed in the cares and the business and the social demands of the world, and a short time before his death, he saw his mistake, and felt that one thing was needful. For years his spiritual life was barely sustained by the prayers of friends and the weekly services of the sanctuary. He might have been a pillar in the Church, but he was only a weight."

ENDNOTES

1   Quoted in *Christianity Today,* November 1994, p. 6.

2   Quoted in *Decision,* December 1981, p. 12.

26
Career Change

Sometimes the kind of commitment we have been describing leads to a change in a person's career. God may call someone out of secular work into full-time service for the Kingdom. But that sentence is a mine field. It needs a lot of qualifying. Otherwise we run into trouble.

First, there is that word *secular*. A common misconception is that our work Monday through Friday is secular; what we do on the Lord's Day is sacred. There doesn't need to be any such dichotomy for the believer. Work at a lathe can be just as sacred as teaching a Bible class if it is done for the glory of God. An office environment can be a sacred place for Christians who witness by their life, by the spoken word, and by the quality of their work. Time spent at the carpenter's bench in Nazareth was just as holy as the three-and-a-half years of Jesus' public ministry. Work can be secular, but it doesn't have to be; no so-called secular work should be the main thing in our life.

The other expression that needs explanation is *full-time service*. Every child of God is a minister in the New Testament sense. Ephesians 4:12 makes it clear that God gave gifts to equip the saints for the work of the ministry. So technically it is not accurate to speak of a segment of the Church as being in full-time ministry. That is a function of all the members. But the fact remains that God calls some to devote their time exclusively to preaching, teaching, and shepherding, and they are supported by gifts from other believers. (I was going to say, "by believers who work for a living," but that would reflect unfavorably on our hard-working missionaries and home workers.)

There is a lot of muddled thinking today on the subject of Christian ministry. When a young man shows an above-average interest in Bible study or a special gift in preaching, the immediate conclusion is that he should go to a seminary and become an ordained minister. Now that some mainline denominations are ordaining women, the thinking spills over in that direction also. This mindset is, first of all, unscriptural. To make seminary training a requisite for Christian service would eliminate Jesus, the disciples, and the apostle Paul. The early Church knew nothing of a humanly-ordained clerical system or of a one-man ministry. Certainly the idea of a female teacher in the church is forbidden by the Word of God (1 Tim. 2:12).

Furthermore, this thinking presents a narrow view of what is meant by ministry. It largely restricts the word to preaching or teaching that is carried on behind a pulpit. The truth is that the word covers any form of service carried on for the Lord. All believers who serve in accordance with the Scripture are ministers regardless of age or gender.

The Lord sometimes calls men and women out of the factory, shop, or office so that they can serve Him without distraction or time limitations. The person goes through a period of soul-searching. What the prophets called "the burden of the Lord" is on him. He is conscious of the Lord speaking to him and laying upon him an ever-increasing spiritual passion. He senses a divine tap on the shoulder. He can't shake it—and he doesn't want to. James Stewart describes that experience like this:

> Once any man has looked into Christ's eyes and felt the magnetism of His way of life, he is never going to be content with the ideals and standards that may have seemed adequate enough before Christ came. Christ has spoiled him for anything else. The old standards of values have become cinders, ashes, dust.

> Peter gave up his career on a day when his net was so filled with

fish that it was breaking. He had to call for help from another boat. Both boats became so full that they began to sink. That is when Jesus said, "Don't be afraid. From now on you will catch men."

Curing Souls, Not Bodies

God's guidance comes in different ways. For example, a Christian might feel increasingly frustrated by the futility of the way he is spending his life. When Dr. Martin Lloyd-Jones gave up a lucrative and prestigious medical practice to preach the gospel, his friends couldn't understand. Let him tell the story:

> People said to me, "Why give up good work—a good profession—after all, the medical profession, why give that up? If you had been a bookie, for instance, and wanted to give that up to preach the gospel, we should understand and agree with you and say that you were doing a grand thing. But medicine—a good profession, healing the sick and relieving pain!" One man even said this, "If you were a solicitor [lawyer] and gave it up, I'd give you a pat on the back, but to give up medicine!" "Ah well," I felt like saying to them, "If you knew more about the work of a doctor, you would understand. We...spend most of our time rendering people fit to go back to their sin!" I saw men on their sick beds, I spoke to them of their immortal souls, they promised grand things. Then they got better and back they went to their old sin! I saw I was helping these men to sin and I decided I would do no more of it. I want to heal souls. If a man has a diseased body and his soul is all right, he is all right to the end; but a man with a healthy body and a diseased soul is all right for sixty years or so and then he has to face an eternity of hell. Ah yes! we have sometimes to give up those things which are good for that which is best of all—the joy of salvation and newness of life.[1]

Another doctor said he laid down his scalpel to concentrate full-time on the instrument that is far more accurate, reliable, and sharper than the latest laser knife, the Word of God.

The chief executive officer of a supermarket chain told a Christian friend he was resigning. When asked why, he replied, "I don't leave at night until after six, and I have to take work home with me. When my business day is over, I have no time or energy left for the things of God. The price in terms of eternity is too big too pay."

Out of the Air Force

Jerry White left the prestigious world of space science and technology to train Christian disciples. He explains:

Full-time Christian work was a career for which I had no interest or inclination. In my early Christian life I had no leading to it, nor was it attractive to me. Yet, about midnight one night in May 1972, I found myself on my knees telling God that I was available, and that I would resign from my career as an Air Force officer to be in full-time Christian work.

Many were critical of my decision. Some were skeptical. One retired officer told me I was 'insane.' My grandmother cried. My wife was initially apprehensive. Most of my relatives were shocked. Others thought that it was a great step of faith. The step seemed illogical, because I had only 6 1/2 year's service left until retirement. Many thought I should wait until then.[2]

When White abandoned his Air Force career to enter full-time work for the Lord, he was marching to the beat of a different drummer. "It wasn't that the grass was greener," he later wrote, "although it was. It wasn't that there was a greater security—although there was. It was just a deepening conviction that God was calling."[2]

Jenny Lind, the famous Swedish opera singer, was converted in New York and soon thereafter decided to leave the stage forever. One day a friend found her sitting on the beach with an open Bible in her lap. The friend asked why she had left such a brilliant career. Jenny replied, "With each passing day, show business made me think less of my Bible and hardly anything at all of what lies beyond this life—so what else could I do?"

A Christian artist had been painting the picture of a poorly dressed young woman clutching a baby to her breast, homeless on a dark street in a raging storm. Suddenly he threw the brush down on the palette and said, "Instead of merely painting the lost, I will go out and save them." That decision led him to Uganda as a missionary.

I always have to chuckle when I think of what C. T. Studd's friends said to him when God called him to the mission field. "You're mad, leaving your cricket and going to be a missionary. Couldn't you wait until you've finished your cricketing days? Couldn't you make more of an impact for God as a cricketer? Why go as a missionary to a place where they have never even heard of cricket?" But Studd was leaving futility in order to find meaning. He was leaving fantasy in order to find reality.

Three believers were sitting at a table, enjoying a meal, and talking about occupations and vocations. One asked the PhD, "What was the subject of your thesis?" He answered, "The hydrodynamic limit for the totally asymmetric simple exclusion process with non-constant speed parameter." After recovering from verbal overload, the third one asked, "What difference does it make?" The PhD, a spiritual, committed disciple of Jesus, thought for a minute. It seemed like a long pause. Then he gave this memorable response: "My inability to answer such questions is the reason I have chosen to leave that field."

Many have made a career change because they felt that they were becoming too much entangled in the affairs of this life. Dr. Alexander Maclaren has written:

> In Paul's time there were no standing armies, but men were summoned from their ordinary avocations and sent into the field. When the hasty call came forth, the plough was left in the furrow, and the web in the loom; the bridegroom hurried from his bride, and the mourner from the bier. All home industries were paralyzed while the manhood of the nation were in the field.[3]

Guy H. King adds his comments to Maclaren's:

> He must not allow himself to get entangled with civilian inter-

ests, when all his energies are supposed to be devoted to the war. He must, for the time, forswear anything, and everything, that would prejudice his soldiering.

A like sacrifice must be seen in the soldier of the Cross. He may find that he will have to give up certain things, certain interests, certain habits, certain amusements, even certain friends—not because any of these are wrong in themselves, but because they are a snare, an entanglement, to him; they get in the way of his success as a soldier.

He will not criticize his fellow Christians if they find no harm in such matters—it is not his business to criticize; though, when asked, he is free to give his opinion, and to explain the reason for his own avoidance. Anything that interferes with our being the best that we can be for Him is to be sacrificed—however harmless it may be to others, and however attractive it may be to ourselves; even though it may be so darling a thing as a hand, or a foot, or an eye (Mt. 18:8-9).

Let it be made clear that there are many things in this life that, for the Christian soldier, are plain duty: family things, social affairs, business matters, that must be attended to—and done all the better for the very reason that he is a Christian. But the point lies in that word 'entangleth': that is where the emphasis rests. When anything, however otherwise legitimate, becomes an entanglement, it must be severely and sacrificially dealt with.[4]

What to Do

When a person is convinced of a divine tap on the shoulder, he should share his concerns with the elders of his church. No man is a sufficient judge of his own spiritual gift or of his fitness for service. The elders will know if he is running away from work, if he has been a failure at everything else, if he is unemployed and looks upon this as a solution.

As we've already seen, in almost every true call of God, there is a measure of human reluctance, a sense of human inadequacy. Moses had it and so did Jeremiah. But the insistent voice of God drowns out such hesitations. There is only one way to go, and that is forward.

So what is the conclusion? Which is better, a secular occupation or full-time Christian work? The answer is that nothing is better than to be in the place of God's choosing, wherever that might be.

But how can we know? There is only one way. That is to yield ourselves to the Lord without reservation. It means to turn over our lives to Him, not just for salvation but also for service. It means to present our bodies to Him as a living sacrifice. When we exchange our will for His, then it is His responsibility to show us exactly what He wants us to do. And when He shows us, the guidance will be so clear that to refuse would be conscious, positive disobedience.

> *I heard Him call—"Come follow!"*
> *That was all.*
> *My earthly gold grew dim,*
> *My heart went after Him,*
> *I rose and followed—*
> *That was all.*
> *Would you not follow*
> *If you heard Him call?*
>
> —Amy Carmichael

A Potential Problem

Sometimes a problem arises when a career change looms on the horizon. The call comes loud and clear to one partner in a marriage, but the other person doesn't hear it. Take the case of a couple who have been serving on the foreign field for fifteen years. Now Glen (only the names are fictitious) feels that the time has come to return home. But Gwen still feels as strongly called to missionary work as ever. She has been an outstanding worker, has mastered the language, has identified with the people, and actually feels more at home on the field than back in the States. What to do? How do they resolve this seeming conflict? (In this case, she submitted to her husband's guidance.)

The conflict could work the other way. It could be that Roy senses the Lord directing him into full-time service, but Ruby does not share his vision. The nesting instinct is strong; she is controlled by the need for security for herself and her children. She has no peace about disturbing the status quo. She is tortured by fears and hesitations.

In seeking a resolution of the problem, it is important to know the degree to which the reluctant spouse is uncommitted. If it is the wife and she is willing to go along with her husband, then that is sufficient authorization for him to make the move. I know of one lady who did not feel that God was calling her to be a missionary, but she was willing to go as a missionary's wife.

If, however, a man's wife is adamantly opposed, then it would be folly for him to make a move. They are one flesh (Eph. 5:31). He must not use Ephesians 5:22 ("Wives, submit to your own husbands, as to the Lord") as a weapon to pressure her into submission. He should respect her spiritual judgment and intuition, realizing that it might be God's way of saving him from a spiritual disaster. And should she make a change unwillingly, she would not be a joyful help to him.

The best thing he can do is to continue in prayer. God is able to bring about a change. The ideal, of course, is when both partners in a marriage are totally committed to work cooperatively and joyfully in pursuing the will of God. The man should pray that the Lord will bring about that kind of unity.

If it does not come, then he should remain in his present work without recriminations, realizing that that is the path ordained for him. The Lord will reward Him for the desire, even if he was not able to see it fulfilled. In the meantime, he should involve himself and his partner in local avenues of service.

It is possible that one spouse not only forbids the other to make a change but is firmly opposed to any involvement whatever by either one in Christian service. This is the worst-case scenario. Apart from divine intervention, life settles down into passive co-existence. Continued prayer is the only option.

A Searching Question

In pondering the whole subject of careers, we should remember a searching question asked by Michael Griffith: "What will we have to show for our life? Will it be measured by life's little rewards and successes, some certificates of education, some silver cups indicative of athletic prowess, a few medals, some newspaper cuttings, promotion within our profession, some status in the local community, a presentation clock on retirement, an obituary notice, and a well attended funeral? Is that all that our life will have meant?"[5]

ENDNOTES

1 From a sermon, *Render therefore unto Caesar the things that are Caesar's; and unto God the things that are God's,* April 28, 1929.

2 *Your Job: Survival or Satisfaction?* Grand Rapids: Zondervan Publishing House, 1977, p. 99.

3 Quoted by Guy H. King, *To My Son,* Fort Washington, PA.: Christian Literature Crusade, 1958, pp. 43-44.

4 Ibid.

5 Documentation unavailable.

Part V
THE EXPERIENCE
OF COMMITMENT

27
It's a Crisis

When we speak of the crisis of commitment, we refer to the first time a person turns over his or her life to the Lord to do with it whatever He wishes. It would be nice to think that this happens at the time of conversion. Sometimes it does, but not always.

Often when a person is saved, he or she knows very little. He can only say, "I was a poor, lost sinner, but Jesus died for me." Or she might say, "Once I was blind, but now I see." Each one nevertheless trusts the Saviour and His finished work for salvation. That is the extent of their present theology.

Then as they grow in the faith, the magnitude of what happened at Calvary begins to dawn on them, and they have an increasing conviction that the Lord Jesus deserves all that they are and have. Even then there may be a struggle to give up personal plans and ambitions. That is why the words *surrender* and *yield* so aptly describe the crisis of commitment.

In making this commitment, an individual is saying to the Lord, "Anywhere you want me to go. Anything you want me to say. Anything you want me to do." And, "Not just a part, or half of my heart, I will give all to Thee." No reservations, nothing less than the whole heart. They realize that it must be everything or nothing because, as Michael Griffith has said, "There is a remarkable all-or-nothing quality about the claims and commands of Christ." From now on, it must be the will of God nothing more, nothing less, nothing else.

When we make that commitment, we know that we are placing our life on the altar as a living sacrifice. And as we do, we can say:

O Son of God, who lov'st me,
I will be Thine alone;
And all I have and am, Lord,
Shall henceforth be Thine own.

—F. R. Havergal

Spurgeon put it this way:

O great and unsearchable God, who knows my heart, and tries all my ways; with a humble dependence on the support of Thy Holy Spirit, I yield up myself to Thee as Thy own reasonable sacrifice, I return to Thee Thine own. I would be forever, unreservedly, perpetually Thine. While I am on earth, I would serve Thee. May I enjoy Thee and praise Thee for ever! Amen.

Hudson Taylor's commitment was similar:

Well do I remember as I put myself, my friends, my all upon the altar, the deep solemnity that came over my soul with the assurance that my offering was accepted. The presence of God became unutterably real and blessed, and I remember...stretching myself on the ground and lying there before Him with unspeakable awe and unspeakable joy. For what service I was accepted I knew not, but a deep consciousness that I was not my own took possession of me which has never since been effaced.

William Borden, Yale 1909, scion of millionaires, forsook all to take the gospel to Muslims. He died in Cairo en route to China at age 26, leaving an impact on the Christian world that is still felt today. This is how he verbalized his commitment:

Lord Jesus, I take hands off as far as my life is concerned. I put Thee on the Throne in my heart. Change, cleanse, use me as Thou shalt choose. I take the full power of Thy Holy Spirit. I thank Thee.

Jim Elliot counted the cost, then prayed:

Father, take my life, yea, my blood, if Thou wilt, and consume it with Thine enveloping fire. I would not save it, for it is not mine to save. Have it, Lord, have it all. Pour out my life as an oblation for the world. Blood is only of value as it flows before Thine altars.

A young woman in South Carolina had a novel way of indicating her commitment. She took a blank sheet of paper and signed her name at the bottom. It was her way of accepting God's will, no matter what it was. She left it to Him to fill in the details.

Now what will happen when a person has made this great renunciation? Some might have an emotional experience. Others may not. But there should be a sense of relief at having done the right thing. There should be assurance that the Saviour has accepted the sacrifice.[1] Beyond that, feelings are not important. What matters is that we have made a firm commitment: "I love my Master. I will not go out free."

It will never occur to us that we have done anything extraordinary. In light of the Cross, we have made no notable sacrifice. We will be able to say:

> *Poor is my sacrifice whose eyes*
> *Are lighted from above.*
> *I offer what I cannot keep,*
> *What I have ceased to love.*
>
> —Anonymous

Finally, we will realize that anything less than full surrender is only "polished sin."

> *Oh, break whatever it may be*
> *That holdeth back my heart from Thee,*
> *Who died my heart to win!*
> *All other love, however dear,*
> *However old, or strong, or near,*
> *Of which Thou art not theme and sphere,*
> *Is only polished sin.*
>
> —Mrs. J. A. Trench

There is a fable that surfaces from time to time and although the details differ, the moral is the same. A party on a hiking expedition came to a river. A voice said to them, "Pick as many pebbles out of the river as you wish, then cross the river and go on. You're going to be glad, and you're going to be sorry." Reactions were mixed. Some picked up as many as they could conveniently carry; they already had a load of camping gear. Others were satisfied with a handful. And still others felt they already had enough sorrow in life; they didn't feel they needed any more.

After they had crossed the river and proceeded a few miles, the pebbles all turned to emeralds. They were glad for all that they had picked, and sorry that they hadn't picked more.

That's just the way it is with commitment. We will be glad for the measure we have turned our lives over to the Saviour. And sorry we hadn't given Him more.

Bye and bye when I look on His face,
Beautiful face, thorn-shadowed face.
Bye and bye when I look on His face,
I'll wish I had given Him more.
More, so much more:
More of my life than I e'er gave before.
Bye and bye when I look on His face,
I'll wish I had given Him more.

Bye and bye when He holds out His hands,
Welcoming hands, nail-pierced hands.
Bye and bye when He holds out His hands,
I'll wish I had given Him more.
More, so much more;
More of my heart than I e'er gave before.
Bye and bye when he holds out His hands,
I'll wish I had given Him more.

Bye and bye when I kneel at His feet,
Beautiful feet, nail-riven feet.

Bye and bye when I kneel at His feet,
I'll wish I had given Him more.
More, so much more;
More of my love than I e'er gave before.
Bye and bye when I kneel at His feet,
I'll wish I had given Him more.

In the light of that beautiful face,
Light from His face, wonderful face.
In the light of that beautiful face,
I'll wish I had given Him more.
More, so much more;
Treasures unbounded for Him I adore.
Bye and bye when I look on His face,
I'll wish I had given Him more.

—Author Unknown

In the late 1970s, the U.S. Navy developed an automatic system for landing planes on an aircraft carrier. The landing control officer would instruct the pilot to line up the plane with the fog-shrouded flight deck. Then as the plane descended, he would say, "Take your hands off the controls." The plane nosed toward the deck, "lurching and shuddering as the computers corrected its course in sync with the carrier's flight deck." The pilot was safe as long as he took his hands off the controls. Otherwise he was inviting a crash.

The Lord is saying to us, "Take your hands off the controls. I will guide you safely home and with a full cargo."

ENDNOTES

1 It should be noted that it is the responsibility of the offerer to be holy (that is, to take sin seriously in one's own life). But even with our best efforts, our hearts cry out: Will He accept my sacrifice? It is a great encouragement to realize that ultimately the acceptance of our sacrifice by God is based on the acceptability of Christ (1 Peter 2:5; Eph. 1:6) *ed.*

28
It's a Process

As has been said, a one time act of commitment is not enough. What began as a crisis must continue as a process. There is to be a once-for-all committal followed by an oft-repeated committal. "The spirit is willing but the flesh is weak." We bravely put our hand to the plow, but then when the cost of discipleship crashes in on us, we look back. That's why John Oxenham wrote:

> *Who answers Christ's insistent call,*
> *Must give himself, his life, his all,*
> *Without one backward look;*
> *Who sets his hand upon the plow,*
> *And glances back with anxious brow,*
> *His calling hath mistook.*
> *Christ claims him, wholly, for His own;*
> *He must be Christ's and Christ's alone.*

The remedy for that tendency to look back is to rededicate ourselves to the Lord Jesus every day. Charlotte Elliott said it in verse:

> *Renew my will from day to day;*
> *Blend it with Thine and take away*
> *All that now makes it hard to say,*
> *"Thy will be done."*

Bishop Taylor Smith used to kneel by his bed every morning and say, "Lord Jesus, this bed your altar, myself your living sacrifice."

Exchange of Wills

Anne Grannis described it as a daily "exchange of wills."

> *I want my life so cleared of self*
> *That my dear Lord may come*
> *And set up His own furnishings*
> *And make my heart His home.*
> *And since I know what this requires,*
> *Each morning while it's still,*
> *I slip into that secret room,*
> *And leave with Him my will.*
> *He always takes it graciously,*
> *Presenting me with His;*
> *I'm ready then to meet the day*
> *And any task there is.*
> *And this is how my Lord controls*
> *My interests, my ills;*
> *Because we meet at break of day*
> *For an exchange of wills.*

Believe He Is Controlling

Then what happens? Probably nothing sensational. If we expect lights to flash, bells to ring, or thrills to vibrate through our nervous system, we will probably be disappointed. What happens is that we go about our normal work without fanfare. Most of it will be routine and some of it menial. If there are tasks we do not particularly enjoy, we do them, knowing that they are part of God's will. We accept whatever he assigns us—accidents, interruptions, or mountain-top experience—as His answer to our commitment.

An English evangelist named Harold Wildish had this helpful advice pasted in the front of his Bible:

As you leave the whole burden of your sin, and rest upon the finished work of Christ [salvation], so leave the whole burden of your life and service, and rest upon the present inworking of the

Holy Spirit [consecration]. Give yourself up morning by morning to be led by the Holy Spirit, and go forth praising and at rest, leaving Him to manage you and your day. Cultivate the habit all through the day of joyfully depending on and obeying Him, expecting Him to guide, to enlighten, to reprove, to teach, to use, and to do in and with you what He wills. Count upon His working as a fact, altogether apart from sight or feelings. Only let us believe in and obey the Holy Spirit as the Ruler of our lives, and cease from the burden of trying to manage ourselves. Then shall the fruit of the Spirit appear in us, as He wills, to the glory of God.

Frances Ridley Havergal offers similar advice once we have turned our lives over to the Lord:

Let us go on our way rejoicing, believing that He has taken our lives, our hands, our feet, our voices, our intellects, our wills, our whole selves, to be ever, only, all for Him. Let us consider it a blessedly settled thing: not because of anything we have felt, or said, or done, but because we know that He hears us, and because we know that He is true to His Word.

Life may not seem sensational on any particular day, but committed disciples will sense that they have a peace and poise in their life that they didn't know before. They will sense that the gears of life are meshing. From time to time they will see things happening that would not happen according to the laws of chance or probability. They will know that God is using them, and yet it is not a knowledge that produces pride. Whether they know it or not, their service sparkles with the supernatural, and when they touch other lives, something happens for God.

Now suppose you have turned your life over to the Lord and every day you renew your vow of commitment to Him. How will you know if He has some important change for you? How will you know when you must start moving in a different direction?

The most important requirement for knowing the will of God is walking in close fellowship with Him. You have to be near to hear. J. N. Darby said, "The first thing in determining the will of God is to be in a right state of soul." This means that you will be confessing and forsaking all known sins as soon as you are aware of them. You will spend time in prayer daily, an indication that you are depending on the Lord rather than on your own intelligence. And by reading, studying, and meditating on the Bible, you will put yourself in the position where God can speak to you.

Guidance does not always come quickly. The Lord teaches us the blessing of waiting on Him. "Faith rests upon the confident assurance that God can speak loudly enough to make a waiting child hear. Our part is to wait quietly until we are sure" (C. I. Scofield).

While you are waiting, it might seem as if nothing is happening, but actually the Holy Spirit is working on your intellect, emotions, and will, so that when the call comes, it is really what you want to do. "It is God who works in you both to will and to do for His good pleasure" (Phil. 2:13).

Here let me share a few pointers that have been helpful to me in the area of divine guidance:

When you are seeking guidance from the Lord and no guidance comes, God's will is for you to stay where you are. Or to put it another way, "Darkness about going is light about staying."

Resist the temptation to manufacture your own guidance: "Look, all you who kindle a fire, who encircle yourselves with sparks: walk in the light of your fire and in the sparks you have kindled—this you shall have from My hand: you shall lie down in torment" (Isa. 50:11). Also resist the temptation to act impulsively: "Do not be like the horse...which must be harnessed with bit and bridle" (Ps. 32:9). If you are really trusting the Lord, you don't have to be in a hurry: "Whoever believes will not act hastily" (Isa. 28:16c).

Wait until the guidance is so clear that to refuse would be positive disobedience. If you sincerely desire to know God's will, you will never miss it.

While waiting, do the things that your hands find to do. A pilot steers a ship when it is in motion. A bicyclist steers the bike when it is moving. So God guides His people when they are doing their duty.

When facing a major change of direction in my life, I ask the Lord to confirm the guidance in two or three different ways. I base this on Deuteronomy 19:15: "By the mouth of two or three witnesses the matter shall be established." If I received only one indication of the Lord's will, I might miss it. But when I have two or three, the guidance is unmistakable.

It often happens that when the divine tap on the shoulder comes, some other attractive alternative appears. It comes as a sort of an escape route, a back-door exit. It might be a satanic ploy to divert you from the path of full obedience. But it probably won't work. You have asked for God's will. He has given it. He has prepared you to want it. So other avenues hold no long-lasting appeal.

Throughout all of life we should be open to a change of direction. Yesterday's guidance is not necessarily today's. Enjoy the thrill of new adventures with God.

That leaves the question of how the Lord will reveal His will. He has an infinite variety of ways. Let me list only a few.

• He guides through the Word of God. First of all, the Scriptures give a general outline of His will. But He also speaks through a specific passage in such a way that it is an unmistakable answer to prayer. Others might not see it, but, to the person seeking guidance, it is unmistakably the voice of God. A fifty-eight-year-old woman was invited to teach in a Christian orphanage in Alaska. She was hesitant to accept because of her age. But one morning the Lord spoke to her through Psalm 39:5: "My age is as nothing before You." She packed up and left for Alaska.

• He speaks through the advice of godly Christians. The elders in the local fellowship should be consulted. They can see pros and cons that may have escaped your notice.

• He speaks through others. Sometimes a seemingly random remark by someone who doesn't know of your exercise of soul strikes home as an indication that the Lord is speaking.

• He speaks through the marvelous converging of circumstances.

The perfect timing of a letter written months before, for example.

• He speaks through hindrances. Paul and his team were forbidden by the Holy Spirit to preach the Word in Asia. Later they tried to go into Bithynia, but the Spirit did not permit them" (Acts 16:6-7). God wanted Paul in Troas where he would receive a vision to cross over to Europe.

• He guides by the example of Christ. "God will never lead us in any course that does not fit the character and teaching of Christ." He never asks us to act irrationally.

• He speaks through the subjective, inward witness of the Holy Spirit. Paul says in Colossians 3:15, "And let the peace of God rule in your hearts…" When we are moving in the right direction and making the right choices, peace will arise in our hearts. If we don't have peace about a certain action, then we should doubt that it is God's will. One of our great Christian writers, J. Oswald Sanders, said, "It is folly to act when the dove of peace has flown from the heart."

One final word of caution. Although feelings may be involved, we should not make a decision based on them alone. Feelings must be confirmed by other factors.

29
Now Then, Do It!

The people of Israel had talked about making David king. Their intentions were good, but they never translated them into action. Finally Abner said to the elders of Israel, "In time past you were seeking for David to be king over you. Now then, do it!" (2 Sam. 3:17-18).

That is God's word for many of His people today. "You have talked about crowning the Lord Jesus Christ as King of your life. You have even sung, 'King of my life I crown Thee now.' You have thought about resigning as ruling monarch and turning over the throne rights to Christ. Now then, do it!"

The time has come. Decision determines destiny. We know that this is true in the matter of salvation. When we receive the Saviour by a definite act of faith, our eternal destiny in heaven is assured. But there is more. When we decide to accept His will for our lives unconditionally, we are assured of a life on earth that fulfills His plan for us.

We have seen that it is a double-barreled decision. First it is a crisis; then it becomes a process. It is a determined beginning that is followed by a continued practice. There is always a first time when we resign as managers of our lives and turn the keys over to Him. But then it must become a daily confirmation of that original decision.

Think of the momentous issues that are involved in the decision. It saves us from time spent out of the will of God, times of wandering in a spiritual desert, time that doesn't count for God. It saves us from a treadmill existence, from trivia, boredom, and nothingness.

On the other hand, an on-going commitment assures us of the luxury of knowing that we are living in the center of His will. It assures us of a life that counts for eternity.

It guarantees the most meaningful life that the wisdom of God can conceive for us. Remember! "He does the very best for those who leave the choice with Him."

It means that at the end of the journey, the heavenly Architect will unroll His blueprint for us, check our life against it, place His nail-scarred hand on our shoulder, and say, "It's just according to plan. Well done, My good and faithful servant." There's nothing better than that.

Life is like a coin. We can spend it any way we want. But we can spend it only once.

Our intentions may be good. We mean well. But that is not enough. We say, "Some day," but God says, "Today." We have been listening to our doubts, fears, excuses, and hesitations too long. Now let us listen to God.

Then let us make this reasonable reply today and every day:

> *Love so amazing, so divine,*
> *Shall have my heart, my life, my all.*

Now then, do it!

ONLY ONE LIFE

Only one life to offer—Jesus, my Lord and King;
Only one tongue to praise Thee and of Thy mercy sing (forever);
Only one heart's devotion, Saviour, O may it be
Consecrated alone to Thy matchless glory,
Yielded fully to Thee.

Only this hour is mine, Lord—may it be used for Thee;
May ev'ry passing moment count for eternity (my Saviour);
Souls all about are dying, dying in sin and shame;
Help me bring them the message of Calv'ry's redemption
In Thy glorious Name.

Only one life to offer—take it, dear Lord, I pray;
Nothing from Thee withholding, Thy will I now obey (my Jesus);
Thou who hast freely given Thine all in all for me,
Claim this life for Thine own to be used, my Saviour,
Ev'ry moment for Thee.

—Avis B. Christiansen